COMMUNICA

GRAMMAR

PRACTICE

Activities for intermediate
students of English

Leo Jones

STUDENT'S BOOK

CAMBRIDGE
UNIVERSITY PRESS

Communicative Grammar Practice is based on the British text
Use of English by Leo Jones, first published in 1985.

Published by the Press Syndicate of the University of Cambridge
The Pitt Building, Trumpington Street, Cambridge CB2 1RP
40 West 20th Street, New York, NY 10011-4211, USA
10 Stamford Road, Oakleigh, Melbourne 3166, Australia

First published 1992
Second printing 1993

Printed in the United States of America

Library of Congress Cataloging-in-Publication Data
Jones, Leo
Communicative grammar practice : activities for intermediate
students of English : student's book / Leo Jones.
     p. cm.
  Includes index.
  ISBN 0-521-39891-6
  1. English language—Grammar 1950—Problems, exercises, etc.
2. English—Textbooks for foreign speakers. I. Title.
PE1112.J58 1992
428.2′4 — dc20
ISBN 0-521-39891-6 (Student's Book)   91-8910
ISBN 0-521-39890-8 (Teacher's Manual)   CIP

Book design: Peter Drucker
Layouts and text composition: M 'N O Production Services, Inc.
Illustrators: Chris Evans, Noel Ford, Mark Kaufman, David McKee, Robert Melendez,
  Wally Neibart, Dave Parkins, Bill Thomson, Sam Viviano

Contents

Contents

Welcome!

Communicative Grammar Practice is a book of activities and exercises. It is for students who have difficulty with English grammar and who make mistakes when they're speaking or writing. The activities and exercises in this book will help you to:

- use English more confidently
- speak and write more accurately
- make fewer mistakes
- review English grammar in an entertaining and interesting way
- express your ideas more clearly
- develop the ability to correct your own mistakes, so that you depend less on being corrected by a teacher

You can't be "taught" to speak and write better English – you have to *learn* it. You can only remember what *you* want to learn, not what I have written in this book or what your teacher tells you. *You* are the most important person in the learning process. If you want to know if something is correct, or if you don't know the meaning of a word, it's up to *you* to find out – by asking your teacher, using a dictionary, or asking a classmate.

Many of the exercises are communicative. They may be more open-ended and less controlled than the grammar exercises or drills you've done before. In English – as in any language – there is rarely just *one* correct way of saying something. Try to experiment with English as you express your ideas and opinions. Don't be afraid to make mistakes – learn from them!

Pair work and *Group work* Doing exercises in groups or in pairs gives everyone in the class a chance to express ideas and share opinions. While this is happening, your teacher can't hear every mistake you make. This means that *you* must pay attention to what your partners are saying, and be ready to suggest corrections. There's no need to correct every little error you notice – only the ones that are *relevant* to the exercise: in other words, mistakes that are connected with the theme of the unit.

Communication activities The communication activities at the back of the book (starting on page 81) give different information to each person in a pair or group. There is an "information gap" between you: Your purpose is to find out what your partner knows and to tell your partner what you know. Related communication activities are on different pages so that you can't see each other's information. The instructions in each unit tell you which activity to turn to at the back of the book.

Grammar summaries These show the main points in each unit, and start on page 66. You can use the summaries for quick reference and review.

I hope you like using *Communicative Grammar Practice!*

1 *Yes / No questions*

1.1   Do you like … ?

A   Work alone. Write two of your favorites (✓) and one thing that you *don't* like (✗) in each category. A few examples are given.

Breakfast   *French toast* ✓   *fresh orange juice* ✓   *strong black coffee* ✗
Snacks   *potato chips* ✓   *vanilla ice cream* ✓   *cheese and crackers* ✗
Meals   *pasta* ✓   *pizza* ✓   **Drinks**
Movies   **Movie stars**
Books   **Colors**
Pieces of music or songs   **Musicians or groups**
Cities   **Sports**

B   *Group work*   Ask questions to find out about the likes and dislikes of the members of your group. For example, your conversation might start like this:

Student A: *Do you like potato chips?*
Student B: *No, I don't. Are potato chips one of your favorite snacks?*
Student C: *Yes they are. I love them. And I like vanilla ice cream too. How about you?*
Student D: *Not really, but I like strawberry. Do you like strawberry too?*

1.2   In the news

A   What questions are the reporters asking in these interviews?

B   *Pair work*   Write ten questions the reporters might ask, beginning with each of these words:

   Do … ?   Does … ?   Have … ?   Has … ?   Are … ?   Is … ?
   Can … ?   Will … ?   Was … ?   Were … ?

For example: *Do you feel proud? Have you done this before?*

C   Now write five more questions beginning with *Did ... ?* Then exchange your list with another pair to compare questions.

D   Change partners and role-play the interviews. Take turns being the reporter.

1.3   Yes or No?

Pair work   Think of four famous people, living or dead – but don't tell your partner who they are.
   Now take turns and ask each other questions to find out who each person is. The only answers you can give are: *Yes*   or   *Yes, in a way.*
                                                                    No   or   *Not exactly.*

1.4   Communication activity: Photographs

Group work   Student A should look at Activity 1 on page 81. Student B looks at Activity 5 on page 82. Student C looks at Activity 12 on page 85.
   Each of you has a different photograph. *Don't* look at each other's pictures. Ask each other *Yes/No* questions to find out about the other pictures.

1.5   Making sure

Look at these examples and then fill in the blanks.

AREN'T YOU ANN'S HUSBAND?

ISN'T SHE BILL'S WIFE?

1. Didn't we meet at Jack's party?
2. Wasn't it Jack who introduced us?
3. Aren't you the one who plays the piano?
4. .... you changed your hairstyle?
5. .... you use to have long hair?
6. .... you wearing a blue sweater that night?
7. .... your car damaged or something?
8. .... you have to leave suddenly?

1.6   Didn't you go to the movies?

A   *Pair work*   Find out quickly what your partner did each day last week. Don't write anything yet. Try to remember what your partner tells you.

B   Now work alone. Make brief notes of what you found out.

C   *Pair work*   Talk to your partner and make sure your notes were correct. For example:

You: *Didn't you go to the movies on Sunday afternoon?*
Your partner: *No, that was Monday. Didn't you play tennis on Monday morning?*
You: *That's right. And didn't you ... ?*

2 | Wh- questions

2.1 Welcome to Earth!

A *Pair work* What questions are the reporters asking?

Examples: *What planet are you from?*
Why did you come to Earth?

B What answers do you think the visitor from outer space might give?

2.2 What did you say?

A Imagine that you are talking on the phone to a friend. Unfortunately it's a bad connection, so you can't hear everything your friend says.
Write down the questions you need to ask your friend whenever you miss some information. For example:

My plane arrives at ▓▓▓▓ p.m.
Question: *What time/when does your plane arrive?*

Hi! Listen: next month I'm going to ▓▓▓▓. Well, I wrote to ▓▓▓▓ and she asked me to visit her. The only problem is that I have to be back home on ▓▓▓▓. The ticket's really cheap: it only costs ▓▓▓▓ round trip! ▓▓▓▓ said she'd meet me at the airport. While I'm there I'd like to go to ▓▓▓▓. I've always wanted to go there because ▓▓▓▓

According to the airline, there are still ▓▓▓▓ seats left. The flight leaves on the ▓▓▓▓ and the return flight is on the ▓▓▓▓. If you can come, you could bring ▓▓▓▓ with you.

B   Use a pencil, not a pen. Write down six sentences about things that happened yesterday. Then erase one piece of information from each sentence.

For example: *I left home at* ████ *in the morning.*

C   *Pair work*   Ask each other questions to find out the missing information.

2.3   I'd like to ask you ...

> *I'd like to ask you . . . how old you are.*
> *Could you tell me . . . when you were born?*
> *Would you mind telling me . . . what you enjoy doing?*

A   Why isn't the interviewer simply asking:
   How old are you?
   When were you born?
   What do you enjoy doing?

Write down five more questions the polite young interviewer might ask.

B   Imagine that you're an inexperienced reporter interviewing a famous person. Role-play the interview with a partner. Be very polite.

2.4   Where were you ...?

A   Complete the questions below in writing.

Detective: Where *...were you on the night of May 13th?*
Suspect: At the movies.

Detective: What ....
Suspect: I don't remember the title.

Detective: When ....
Suspect: Oh, about 11 o'clock, I guess.

Detective: Who ....
Suspect: No one. I went alone.

Detective: Where ....
Suspect: I went right home.

Detective: What ....
Suspect: At midnight.

B   Write four more questions the detective should ask.

3 *The past:* What happened?
The present perfect: What has happened?

3.1 Communication activity: Have you ever...?

Have you ever ridden a horse?
                    Yes, I have.
When was that?
                    I rode one last summer.
What was it like?
                    Oh, it was awful.
Why? What happened?
                    I fell off and hurt my back. What
                    about you? Have you ever...

Pair work   Student A should look at Activity 3, while Student B looks
at Activity 9. Both activities are at the back of the book. You'll be finding out
about some of your partner's achievements.

3.2 Go–went–gone

A *Pair work*   Fill in the blanks in this table of regular and irregular
verbs:

Base form	Past tense	Past participle	Base form	Past tense	Past participle
beat	beat	*beaten*	lay	....	....
bite	....	bitten	....	lay	....
....	....	blown	....	lied	....
....	caught	....	....	led	....
choose	....	....	....	left	....
drive	....	....	live	....	....
eat	....	....	lose	....	....
....	fell	....	....	rose	....
feel	....	....	steal	....	....
....	....	flown	....	....	torn
....	hid	....	....	....	thrown
....	....	held	wear	....	....

B   Write sentences using 10 of the verbs above. Use each one in three
different ways, like this:

*She often **loses** her temper.*   *He sometimes **feels** embarrassed.*
*He **lost** his way in the dark.*   *She **felt** something cold crawling up her leg.*
*I've **lost** my front door key.*   ***Have** you **ever felt** lonesome?*

6

3.3 Have you done that yet?

A *Pair work*   Look at this list of things that your friend Tony was planning to do today. He's checked (✓) the things he's done so far. Talk about the things he's already done and the things he hasn't done yet. For example:

"He hasn't called the travel agency yet."   *"He's already bought some bread."*

```
call the travel agency              buy some bread ✓
arrange to meet Sandy for dinner ✓  make dinner reservations
do yesterday's homework ✓           do today's homework
wash the car                        fill the car with gas ✓
write to parents                    buy birthday card for Mom ✓
read today's newspaper ✓            watch the news on TV
```

B *Pair work*   Tell your partner about the things you have already done today and some things you haven't done yet. Find out what time your partner did each of the things. For example:

Your partner: *I've already had breakfast, but I haven't had lunch yet.*
You: *What time did you have breakfast?*

3.4 Communication activity: Famous people

Pair work   Student A should look at Activity 2, and Student B at Activity 15. You will be talking about some famous people of the past.

3.5 One fine day

A *Group work*
The pictures in this cartoon strip are printed in the wrong order. Decide how to rearrange them to make a complete story.

B *Pair work*   Tell your story to a member of a different group.

C   Write your version of the story.

7

4 *The past continuous:* What was happening?
The present perfect continuous:
What has been happening?

4.1 What were you doing?

A What answers do you think the man gave in the cartoons on the right?

B What's the difference in meaning between each of these sentences:

She was having dinner when her husband came home.
She had dinner when her husband came home.
She had already had dinner when her husband came home.

He went to the store when the sun came out.
He was going to the store when the sun came out.
He had already been to the store when the sun came out.

C Fill in the blanks, using your own ideas:

1. We .... on the patio when it started to rain.
2. They .... along slowly when a deer ran across the road.
3. She .... the book when she fell asleep.
4. He .... the letter when his wife came into the room.
5. I .... some coffee when the lights went out.
6. She .... the window when the phone rang.

4.2 When the phone rang ...

Write sentences using the words below. Look at the example first.

1. When the doorbell rang ... (*home, TV*)
   When the doorbell rang, I was sitting at home watching TV.

2. When the lights went out ... (*armchair, book*)
3. When my alarm clock went off ... (*bed, summer vacation*)
4. When my guests arrived ... (*kitchen, dinner*)
5. When I met my old friend ... (*park, flowers*)
6. When the rain started ... (*beach, picnic*)
7. When they called me for the meeting ... (*desk, working*)
8. When the phone rang ... (*window, view*)

4.3   How long have you been … ?

I guess I'm a little late. Have you been waiting long?
      Yes. I've been waiting here since 7:00.
That means you've been waiting for over an hour! I'm really sorry!

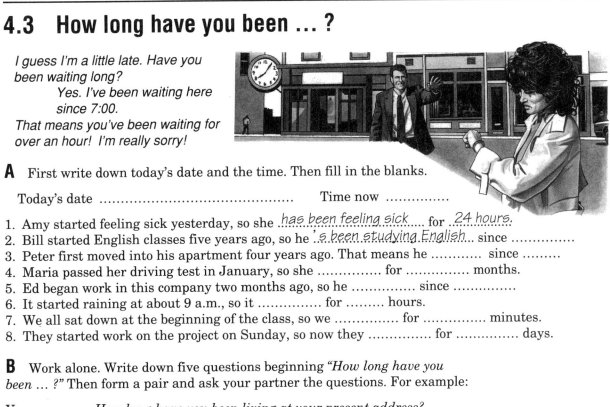

A   First write down today's date and the time. Then fill in the blanks.

Today's date ……………………………………   Time now ……………

1. Amy started feeling sick yesterday, so she *has been feeling sick* for *24 hours.*
2. Bill started English classes five years ago, so he *'s been studying English* since ……………
3. Peter first moved into his apartment four years ago. That means he ………… since ………
4. Maria passed her driving test in January, so she …………… for …………… months.
5. Ed began work in this company two months ago, so he …………… since ……………
6. It started raining at about 9 a.m., so it …………… for ……… hours.
7. We all sat down at the beginning of the class, so we …………… for …………… minutes.
8. They started work on the project on Sunday, so now they …………… for …………… days.

B   Work alone. Write down five questions beginning *"How long have you been … ?"* Then form a pair and ask your partner the questions. For example:

You: *How long have you been living at your present address?*
Your partner: *Oh, let me think … we moved there about five years ago.*
You: *So you've been living there since …*

4.4   I looked out the window…

Imagine that this was the view from your window when you got up this morning. Write a paragraph describing all the things that were happening.

5 *Past, present, and future*

5.1 A woman alone

Group work Look at the
picture and decide together
what has just happened – and
what is going to happen next.

5.2   Communication activity: What's going on?

Pair work   Student A should look at Activity 20, and Student B at 31.
You'll be describing a scene to your partner.

5.3   What has happened?

Pair work   What do you think has happened to each person shown here?
What do you think is going to happen next?

5.4 Communication activity: Those were the days!

Pair work   Imagine that you and your partner are old friends. You haven't seen each other for five years. Student A should look at Activity 35, and Student B at 48. You'll be talking about the things you used to do.

5.5 Before TV

A *Group work*   Discuss these questions:

What did people use to do before
  they had television?
How did they spend their free time?
How has TV changed people's lives?
Without TV, how would your own
  life be different?
How will TV continue to change
  people's lives in the future?

B *Group work* Ask and answer similar questions about the following inventions and discoveries we now depend on:

airplanes	tape recorders	plastic	microwave ovens
electric lights	cars	computers	vaccinations

Think of some other inventions and discoveries we now take for granted.

C   Write a paragraph describing the most interesting points that were made in your group.

6 Quantity

6.1 Countable or uncountable?

COUNTABLE: A ....   one ....   two ....s   several ....s
not many ....s   fewer ....s
UNCOUNTABLE: Not much ....   less ....

A *Pair work*   Put a C beside the words below that are countable and a U beside the ones that are uncountable. You can check this by finding out if they fit into the blanks above. The first ones are done for you as examples.

money U   *dollar* C   *cash* U   *advice* U   *scenery* U   *election* C
English   *food*   *furniture*   *gas*   *health*   *honey*   *job*   *journey*
language   *magazine*   *meal*   *meat*   *news*   *oil*   *paint*   *pasta*
progress   *rain*   *rice*   *river*   *safety*   *salt*   *snow*   *storm*   *table*
travel   *trip*   *vocabulary*   *water*   *weather*   *wine*   *word*   *work*

B Write six sentences using words you got wrong or words you had to find out the meanings of.

6.2 So much! So many!

A Use both of the words in the parentheses to make two sentences with *so much* or *so many*.

1. They have *so many possessions/ so much money* that everyone envies them.   (*possession, money*)
2. I received .... that I couldn't decide what to do.   (*suggestion, advice*)
3. I had to learn .... that I got a splitting headache.   (*information, facts*)
4. The professor wants to do .... that she needs a new laboratory.   (*experiment, research*)
5. We had to do .... that we didn't finish till midnight.   (*homework, exercise*)
6. I had to carry .... that my arms were aching.   (*luggage, bag*)
7. We've heard .... that we know everything about it now.   (*report, news*)
8. This encyclopedia contains .... that you don't need any other books.   (*information, article*)

B Add your own endings to these sentences:

1. During our vacation we had .... fun that ....
2. The students in this class have made .... progress that ....
3. I made .... mistakes on the test that ....
4. There was .... traffic that ....
5. In English there seems to be .... vocabulary that ....
6. And there seem to be .... exceptions to every grammar rule that ....

6.3 Communication activity: How much? How many?

A *Pair work* First, match the items below.

1. a bar of	......	beer
2. a bottle of	......	bread
3. a box of	......	cake
4. a cube of	......	soap
5. a jar of	......	candy
6. a loaf of	......	cigarettes
7. a pack of	......	honey
8. a slice of	......	ice

9. a box of	....	soda
10. a can of	....	matches
11. a packet of	....	milk
12. a pot of	....	paper
13. a carton of	....	sugar
14. a pitcher of	....	tea
15. a sheet of	....	toothpaste
16. a tube of	....	water

B *Pair work* Now Student A should look at Activity 8 while Student B looks at 39.

6.4 Spot the errors

Pair work Find the mistakes in these sentences and correct them.

```
1.  How many furniture is there in your apartment?
2.  Can you give me an information about flight to Tokyo?
3.  Hurry up! We don't have many times before the show starts.
4.  This tabletop is made of a glass, and the legs are made of a wood.
5.  I have to write a letter. Can you lend me a paper and an envelope?
6.  He's going to have his hairs cut and his beards trimmed.
7.  I drink tea without a milk but with slice of lemon and a sugar.
8.  There's fewer traffic downtown today than day before yesterday.
```

6.5 A few dollars more...

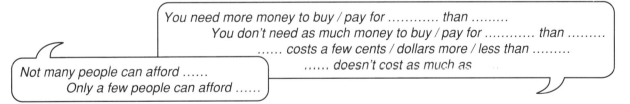

You need more money to buy / pay for .... than ....
You don't need as much money to buy / pay for .... than ....
...... costs a few cents / dollars more / less than ....
...... doesn't cost as much as ......

Not many people can afford ......
Only a few people can afford ......

Pair work Decide how much money you'd have to spend to pay for these things. Use the expressions above.

a vacation ...	in the Caribbean	in Europe	in Canada	in Taiwan
a bus or subway ride...	downtown	to the beach	to your home	to the airport
a taxi ride ...	downtown	to the train station	to the stadium	to the airport
an airplane ticket ...	to Hong Kong	to Hawaii	to Puerto Rico	to San Francisco
a ticket for ...	a movie	the opera	a lottery	a parking lot the art museum
a stamp for ...	a letter to Mexico	a postcard to Japan	a letter to Brazil	

a newspaper   a cup of coffee   a candy bar   a TV guide magazine   a ballpoint pen
a compact disc   a cassette   a record album   a videocassette

7 Articles – I

7.1 Do you like fruit?

A Fill in the blanks in this conversation with *a, an, the,* or Ø *:

A: *Would you like .... apple?*
B: *Oh, yes please! I love .... apples.*
A: *Well, there's .... big one and .... small one.*
B: *Oh, I'll have .... small one please.*
A: *Are you sure you won't have .... big one?*
B: *No, thanks. Mmm! What .... delicious apple!*
A: *Glad you like it. I guess I'll have .... big one myself.*

B *Pair work* Act out similar conversations about another kind of fruit:

bananas   oranges   peaches   pears   apricots   plums   figs   dates

C Make general statements about your likes and dislikes of the things listed below. Use sentences like these:

I usually like apples because .... , but the apple I had yesterday was ....
Usually I hate bananas because .... , but the banana I tried just now was ....
As a rule I love coffee because .... , but the coffee they serve here is ....

apples	olives	sandwiches	eggs	toast	chocolate
lemons	raisins	cookies	tea	rice	fish
pineapples	cake	hamburgers	coffee	butter	steak

7.2 Fill in the blanks

Fill in the blanks with *a, the,* or Ø.* The first is done for you as an example.

1. ..*Ø*.. Automobiles and ..*Ø*.. trucks cause ..*Ø*.. air pollution, which damages *the*. environment.
2. .... pollution caused by .... cars is worse if .... cars are driven at .... high speeds.
3. I was watching .... great movie on .... TV .... last night when .... TV stopped working.
4. .... movie I saw was awfully violent – I don't like .... violent movies.
5. .... good health and .... happiness are more important than .... wealth or .... power.
6. .... Washington is .... capital city of .... United States, but .... New York is .... city with .... largest number of .... inhabitants in .... country.
7. .... Italian food is great, but .... pizza I had at .... restaurant on .... corner was terrible.
8. She is studying .... history and .... geography – her special interests are .... history of .... Latin America and .... geography of .... Canada.

* Ø means "nothing" – no article is used.

14

7.3 Communication activity: How do you feel about ...?

Pair work   Student A should look at Activity 4, while Student B looks at
11. Find out your partner's views on the subjects listed in your activity.

A: How do you feel about watching TV?
B: I think watching TV every evening
   is a waste of time – there are more
   enjoyable things you can do.
A: Such as?
B: Such as meeting friends, reading a
   book, listening to music. What do
   you think?
A: Well, I think TV can often be
   interesting and informative.

7.4 What a job!

A *Pair work*   Can you explain what all of these people do?

author   carpenter   conductor   farmer   flight attendant   movie actor
nurse   parent   pianist   pilot   professor   waiter

Example: *An architect is a person who designs buildings.*   OR
            Architects are people who design buildings.

Would you rather be a child or an adult?
– I think I'd rather be a child.
Why?
– Because children don't have to worry about . . .

B *Pair work*   Follow the pattern above to talk about these people.

doctor   *or* patient   officer   *or* soldier
teacher   student   referee   player
driver   passenger   millionaire   poor person
clerk   customer   tour guide   tourist
employer   employee   actor   member of the audience

*Are you going
to be a writer?
Or maybe a TV
reporter?*

C *Pair work*   Here are the subjects these students are studying now.
What jobs or professions do you think they're going to have when they get out
of school?

Ann: medicine   Ed: cooking
Tim: sociology   Sue: Spanish
Ellen: history   Bill: business
Jack: music   Maria: creative writing
Jane: law   Ron: computer science

*I'm studying
journalism.*

Example: Q: *What's Lisa going to do when she gets out of school?*
           A: *Maybe she's going to be a writer. Or perhaps a TV reporter?*

8 Articles – II

8.1 Place names

A *Pair work*   Add *three* more examples to each of these lists.

ISLAND GROUPS   the West Indies, the Philippines, ...
MOUNTAIN GROUPS   the Andes, the Rockies, ...
OCEANS & SEAS   the Atlantic, the Mediterranean, ...
RIVERS   the Amazon, the Mississippi, ...
HOTELS   the Waldorf Astoria, the Hilton, ...
MUSEUMS & GALLERIES   the Metropolitan Museum, the National Gallery, ...

COUNTRIES* Japan, Brazil, ...   STATES Texas, Florida, ...
CONTINENTS Africa, Antarctica, ...   CITIES Toronto, Buenos Aires, ...
MOUNTAINS   Mount Fuji, Mt. Everest, ...   LAKES Lake Michigan, Lake Victoria, ...
ISLANDS   Bermuda, Honshu, ...
STREETS   Wall Street, Park Avenue, Sunset Boulevard, ...
IMPORTANT PLACES IN A CITY OR REGION: San Diego Zoo, Disneyland, Chinatown,
            Grand Central Station, ...

* Notice the use of *the*: the USA / the United States of America   *but* America
the Republic of China   *but* Taiwan   the USSR / the Soviet Union   *but* Russia
the Netherlands   *but* Holland   the People's Republic of China   *but* China
the UK / the United Kingdom   *but* Britain / Great Britain

B *Group work*   Ask your partners:
   Which of the places in the lists above would you like to visit? Why?
   Which places would you *not* like to visit? Why not?

8.2 The eighties

Rewrite these newspaper headlines as complete sentences.

1980   Eruption of Mt. St. Helens in Washington State causes $2.7 billion in damage
In 1980, the eruption of Mt. St. Helens in Washington State caused $2.7 billion in damage.
1981   Weather perfect for wedding of Charles and Diana in St. Paul's Cathedral in London
1982   Compact discs go on sale in record stores for first time
1983   Sales of Michael Jackson's *Thriller* album reach 37 million
1984   Archbishop Desmond Tutu of South Africa wins Nobel Peace Prize
1985   Mikhail Gorbachev becomes leader of Soviet Union
1986   Accident at nuclear power station in Chernobyl
1987   Painting by van Gogh sold for $53.9 million in auction in London
1988   Total production cost of *Rambo III* is $58 million; most expensive film ever made
1989   Berlin Wall opens for first time

16

8.3　In bed

Fill in the blanks below with *a, an, the,* or *Ø*.*

1. If you have ...<u>a</u>... cold, do you go to ...<u>Ø</u>... bed or go to ...<u>Ø</u>... work as usual?
2. Would you like to eat .... lunch at .... cafe next door, or go to .... new restaurant downtown?
3. If you want to learn .... language, is it better go to .... school or use .... dictionary?
4. Do you usually eat .... lot for .... lunch, or do you just have .... snack?
5. If you look out of .... window in .... room you're in now, what can you see?
6. What kind of .... music do you like best: .... jazz, ... rock, or .... classical music?
7. Do you know anyone who has been to .... United Kingdom, ... China, or .... Soviet Union?
8. Do you come to .... class by .... car, on .... foot, or on .... bus?

8.4　Spot the errors

Pair work　Each sentence below has two errors in it. Correct the mistakes you find.

1. I love a mountains, and I enjoy a seashore too.
2. I have the headache and I need a aspirin.
3. I don't like talking on telephone — I prefer to write the letters.
4. He's the very good friend of mine, even though he has the bad temper.
5. She's studying the music because she wants to become professional musician.
6. I'm going to watch a TV tonight to see a movie about the Brazil.
7. I read in newspaper that we're going to have a cold weather.
8. When a police arrived, all the people in building were questioned.

8.5　A writer's life

Fill in the blanks with *a, an, the,* or *Ø*.*

As .... writer, I seem to spend .... most of .... time working in my office at .... home, sitting alone in front of .... computer. In fact, ... only people I see regularly are .... members of my family when they get home from .... work or .... school. Otherwise, I don't have much contact with .... people, and I'm sorry that I haven't kept in .... touch with .... friends I made at .... college. I often get .... letters and .... phone calls from .... people at .... publisher's, though, and I try to get out of .... house at least once .... day. From .... time to time I give .... lectures or teach .... courses at .... conferences in .... North America or abroad. But if I ever run out of .... ideas or I start suffering from .... loneliness, I'll give up .... writing .... books. Then maybe I'll start .... new career where I work with lots of .... people and I can have .... conversation whenever I feel like .... one!

* *Ø means "nothing" – no article is used.*

9 Comparison

9.1 Braver than a lion!

A *Pair work* Make a list of all the animals in the picture in order of size, from the largest down to the smallest.

B Decide together which of the animals in the picture is the:

fastest – slowest	fiercest – most gentle
rarest – most common	ugliest – most beautiful

9.2 More exciting than knitting!

I think sewing is a lot more difficult than knitting!

Well, I think it's much less difficult.

Anyhow, neither of them is as difficult as learning English.

Group work Look at the activities listed below. Decide together which is:

the most exciting	*the dullest*	*the most expensive*	*the most dangerous*	*the safest*
the most energetic	*the most relaxing*	*the most rewarding*	*the most mindless*

butterfly collecting	cooking	dancing	sewing
learning a foreign language	cycling	mountain climbing	skiing
watching television	knitting	parachuting	gambling
playing the piano	reading	playing tennis	fishing
stamp collecting	walking	scuba diving	swimming

18

9.3 It's the most...

Group work What can you say about each of these things, using *the most...* or *the -est*?

Sue's the tallest.
Maria's the youngest.
Jim's the most intelligent.
Ted's the oldest.

apple   grapefruit   pineapple   lemon
Paris   Tokyo   London   New York
sports car   jeep   station wagon   limousine
bicycle   motorcycle   train   camel
milk   soda   iced tea   orange juice
January   April   July

For example: *A pineapple is the sweetest fruit.*
A grapefruit is the juiciest fruit.

9.4 It's much too big!

Group work Write *four* sentences about each of the cartoons. For example:

The van isn't big enough for the elephant.
An elephant is such a big animal that it won't fit in a van.

The elephant's too big to get in the van.
He's so big that we'll have to get a truck.

9.5 In other words ...

Rewrite each sentence starting with the words on the right.

1. No one I know is taller than he is.   He's ... *the tallest person I know.*
2. No one has ever said such a nice thing to me.   That's the ...
3. I can't walk that far with my bad leg.   It's ...
4. A Boeing 747 holds more passengers than a 727.   A Boeing 727 ...
5. I prefer coffee to tea.   I think coffee ...
6. This shirt is too dirty for me to wear.   This shirt isn't ...
7. It isn't as warm in Canada as it is in Mexico.   Mexico is a ...
8. There are fewer people in Taiwan than in Korea.   The population of Korea ...

19

10 | Requests and obligation

10.1 Would you mind...?

Would you mind ... ?   No, of course not.
Could you ... ?   Yes, of course.
Can you ... please?   Certainly.
I'd like you to ...   All right.

Would you mind if I ... ?   Not at all.
Do you mind if I ... ?   No, of course not.
May I ... ?   Yes, of course.
Is it all right if I ... ?   Go right ahead.
Could I ... ?   Sure.

What would you say in these situations? Use the expressions above.

The door is locked.	The room is too dark.
You are hungry.	Your suitcase is too heavy.
You feel tired.	You can't do your homework.
You are cold.	You want to make a phone call.
You need a dictionary.	You feel hot and sweaty.

10.2 Communication activity: I'd like you to ...

I'd like you to ...   All right.
I want you to ...   OK.
Can you ... ?   Of course.
Will you please ... ?   Sure. No problem.

Pair work   Student A should look at Activity 13,
while Student B looks at 21. You'll be asking your partner
to do various things, using the expressions shown here.

10.3 Make yourself at home!

Pair work   Imagine that a very easygoing friend is coming to stay with
you, but your roommate is very strict about neatness, smoking, noise, etc.
Complete each of these sentences with advice for your friend:

You can ...	It's all right to ...	You'd better not ...	You're allowed to ...
You can't ...	If you want you can ...	You aren't supposed to ...	You aren't allowed to...

Example: *You can watch TV, but you can't watch it after 10 p.m.*

10.4 Enjoy your flight!

A *Group work*   Decide together which of the following things can be carried onto an airplane, in addition to one small carry-on bag.

umbrella	skis	radio	magazines	guitar
binoculars	a pet	camera	a plant	child's stroller
coat	briefcase	handbag	sandwiches	laptop computer

For example: *You're allowed to take an umbrella.*

B *Group work*   Now decide which of the following activities are permitted or forbidden on a plane:

drinking	smoking	opening doors and windows	playing ball
eating	standing up	undoing your seatbelt	reading
running	sleeping	walking around	singing

10.5 Do I have to…?

Do I have to … ?
Is it necessary to … ?
Should I … ?
Do I need to … ?

You don't have to …
You can't …
There's no need to …
You don't need to …
You have to …
You've got to …
You ought to …
It's a good idea to …

Group work   Imagine that you're talking to a foreigner who is going to visit your country for the first time. Think of questions a foreigner might ask. Take turns giving advice about the habits a foreigner would have to get used to. Talk about some of these things:

Getting into the country: crossing the border, passport, customs, visa, vaccinations
Transportation: public transportation, driving a car, taking taxis, cycling
Shopping: kinds of stores, finding bargains, paying with cash or a credit card
Eating: restaurants, cafes, table manners, meal times
Social behavior: meeting strangers, visiting people at home, inviting people out
Language: where English can be used, where your own language must be used
Gestures: different meanings of gestures in your country and other countries

10.6 In other words …

Rewrite each of these sentences using phrases you've learned in this unit.

1. You can't chew gum in class.   You aren't ....
2. Is it necessary for me to attend every class?   Do I ....
3. Can I bring my dog to class?   Is ....
4. Please open your books to page 13.   I ....
5. You don't have to wear a suit for school. There ....
6. Could I leave early today?   Would ....
7. Could you pass out these books please?   Would ....
8. Exams are not mandatory.   You don't ....

11 | *Ability*

11.1   Evening classes

Imagine that you decided to enroll in each of the classes advertised above.
  What would you say before you enrolled?
  What would you think during the first class?
  What would you be able to say proudly at the end of the course?

Pair work   Which of the courses would you *really* like to take? Add some more courses that you'd like to take.

11.2   Communication activity: Shopping lists

Pair work   Student A should look at Activity 23, while Student B looks at 28.

You'll be talking about the items on your shopping lists that you were able or unable to get.

a dozen large eggs
1 bag of carrots
1 jar of grape jelly
2 small loaves of
    whole wheat bread
2 pounds of cheese
1 jar of instant coffee
3 large cans of soup

1 large roll of Scotch tape
1 box of paper clips
2 cassettes (C90)
2 red ballpoint pens
4 size AA batteries
1 pack of airmail envelopes
1 large box of staples

List 1   *List 2*

11.3 Success at last!

She was able to ...
She managed to ...
He wasn't able to ...
He couldn't ...
He didn't manage to ...

A Write sentences about the scenes in the cartoons using the structures above. For example:

He didn't manage to open the door. or *He wasn't able to open the door.*

B Write sentences about three things you were able to do recently *and* three things you tried to do but didn't manage to do successfully.

11.4 Do-it-yourself

A *Pair work*   Which of the jobs shown here can you do without help? Be honest! Use the phrases below.

I can do that myself.
I'd need someone to help me.
I'd get someone to help me do that.
I'd have ...... do that for me.
I'd get ...... to do that for me.
I don't know how to ...
I wish I could ...

paint a ceiling	change the oil in a car
tune a piano	change a flat tire
build new shelves	sew on a button
replace a fuse	iron a shirt
change a light bulb	bake a cake
install an air conditioner	send a fax
replace a broken window	fix a broken TV
repair a cassette recorder	write a letter on
fix a burst water pipe	a word processor

Example: *"I'd have a plumber fix a burst water pipe for me. I couldn't do that myself. What about you? Can you fix a burst water pipe?"*

B Write five sentences about things that your partner can do.

Example: *John can repair a cassette recorder.*

12 Advice and suggestions

12.1 What should I do?

What should I do?
Should I ... or ... ?
Is it worth ...-ing ...?
I can't decide whether to ... or ...
I'm wondering whether to ... or ...
Would it be a good idea to ...?
Do you think I ought to ... or ...?

A *Pair work*   You want some advice on the topics below. Write down
your questions, using different expressions from above.

Take bus or taxi to work?

Vacation: stay home or go abroad?

This evening: go out or watch TV?

This weekend: stay home and study or visit a friend?

Car: buy used car or new one?

Hair: get it cut or let it grow?

Restaurant tonight: order chicken or fish?

B   Write down some more topics you'd like
advice on. Then ask your partner's advice.

12.2 If I were you...

If I were you ...   *You should ...*
I think you ought to ...   *You'd better ...*
Why don't you ... ?   *You could ...*
I'd advise you to ...   *My advice is to ...*

What advice would you give Joe? For example:

If I were you, I'd buy some new clothes.   or
You'd better buy some new clothes.

12.3 If you ask me…

A Imagine that your friend is having trouble at work and is thinking of looking for another job. You think it's a mistake to leave a good job. What would you say to your friend, using these expressions?

I don't think you ought to …   *You shouldn't …*
It isn't a good idea to …   *It'd be better not to …*
If I were you I wouldn't …   *I don't advise you to …*

B *Pair work* Suppose another friend is thinking of doing these things. What advice would you give?

swimming from France to England   opening a vegetarian restaurant
taking up hang gliding   buying a compact disc player
writing an autobiography   emigrating to Australia
getting married   becoming a teacher

12.4 That's easier said than done

Group work Each of you plays the role of one of the people shown below. Ask your partners for their advice. You can turn down the advice you don't like by saying:
That's easier said than done, because …   or   *That's a good idea, but …*

12.5 People with problems

Imagine that you were sent these letters by friends.

A *Pair work*
Decide what advice you'd give to each friend.

B Write a reply to one of the letters.

and I've become so dependent on them that I can't give them up. Yesterday I smoked three whole packs! I just don't have any will power.
What do you think I should do?
Best,
Chris

and my boss wants me to move to New York and take over our American branch. This would mean leaving all my friends and starting a new life.
    Maybe I should tell my boss that I'm not interested in a promotion. What do you think?

Yours,
Lee

13 | *Doing* or *to do? – I*

13.1 It's easy to...

A Complete the sentences below using *-ing* . . . in one sentence and *to* . . .
in the other.

1. I love to go the movies.
   ...*Going to the movies*... is great.   It's fun ...*to go to the movies.*.......
2. I can easily write a 150-word composition.
   .... is easy.   It isn't hard ....
3. I like going to the beach on weekends.
   .... is enjoyable.   It's nice ....
4. I get embarrassed when I meet strangers.
   .... is embarrassing.   It's embarrassing for me ....
5. I can't stand it when I'm criticized.
   .... is awful.   It's terrible ....

B Now write five more sentences like the ones above. This time write
about your own feelings and opinions.

13.2 Without blinking

A Fill in the blanks in these sentences.

1. It's impossible to sneeze without ......*closing*...... your eyes.
2. I had an upset stomach after .... oysters.
3. Are you interested in .... to the beach with us?
4. I'd like to go to Europe, but I'm afraid of ....
5. We were very disappointed about .... the game.
6. I drove very fast, but I didn't succeed in .... the plane.
7. Thank you very much for .... me such a nice gift.

B *Pair work*   Complete these sentences together. Then ask
another pair to answer your questions.

1. Can you keep your eyes open for a whole minute ...*without*........
   ...*blinking once?*...
2. Can you touch your toes without ...
3. Can you stop hiccups by ...
4. Can you cure a cold by ...
5. Can you write a letter in English without ...
6. Do you always brush your teeth after ...
7. Do you ever make notes before ...

13.3 Verbs + *-ing* or *to* …

A Look at these verbs that are usually followed by *-ing*:
dislike   enjoy   finish   give up   go on   can't help   keep   miss   put off

And these verbs that are usually followed by *to* . . . :
can't afford   choose   decide   expect   forget   hope   intend   learn
would like   manage   didn't mean   pretend   promise
allow someone   encourage someone   help someone   invite someone   teach someone

B Rewrite each sentence using the words on the right.

1. Smoking is bad for your health, you know. *(give up)* *You ought to give up smoking.*
2. He was wearing a police officer's uniform. *(pretend)*
3. That new video is too expensive for us to buy. *(can't afford)*
4. I don't like to watch TV every night. *(dislike)*
5. I'm going to write those letters tomorrow, not today. *(put off)*
6. I think about my problems all the time. *(can't help)*
7. I want to ask them to visit our home. *(invite)*
8. I'm sorry I stepped on your foot. *(didn't mean)*
9. I'm sad that I'm not with my family. *(miss)*
10. They interrupt the class all the time. *(keep)*

C *Pair work*   Complete each sentence using your own ideas.

1. Time ran out before we had finished *writing our answers to the quiz.*
2. After finishing their meal, they decided …
3. Because of the fog at the airport, we expect …
4. We asked them to be quiet, but they went on …
5. You have to take driving lessons if you want to learn …
6. The boxes were so heavy that I couldn't manage …
7. My favorite teacher in school used to encourage us …
8. I'm sorry, I forgot …

13.4 I prefer…

These verbs can be used either with *-ing* or with *to*. . . , with the same meaning:

begin   continue   hate   like   love   prefer   can't stand   start   try

A Rewrite these sentences using the verbs on the left.

1. *love*   She thinks golf is a great game to play.
2. *start*   We were at the beach when the rain began.
3. *hate*   He doesn't like taking showers at all!
4. *begin*   She felt better after taking her medicine.
5. *continue* I don't know if I want to study math again next year.

B *Group work*   What things do you love, like, or hate doing (or to do)? And what do you enjoy or dislike doing? Tell your partners.

14 Doing or to do? – II

14.1 Looking forward to...

I'm not looking forward to getting up early.

A *Group work* Imagine that you're talking about a friend who is about to start taking English classes:

What do you think your friend is **looking forward to** doing?
What do you think he or she is **not looking forward to** doing?
What will your friend have to **get used to** doing?
What do you think your friend may **object to** doing?

B Write down the five best ideas your group has thought of.

14.2 Communication activity: Stop!

We stopped to eat our lunch.
We stopped eating our lunch when it started to rain.
We waited under a tree till it stopped raining.

Pair work Look at the examples above. Then Student A should look at Activity 10, and Student B at 17. This communication activity is in two parts.

14.3 Communication activity: Don't forget!

> *I'm really sorry, but I forgot to bring my wallet. I remember seeing it on the hall table earlier, but I didn't remember to bring it with me.*

Pair work   Student A should look at Activity 16, and Student B at 26. Again, make sure that you do both parts of this activity.

14.4 Ric Rules

> We aren't allowed to walk on the grass.

> They won't even let us sit on the grass!

> Yes, it's too bad we aren't allowed to sit on the grass.

KEEP OFF THE GRASS

SCHOOL RULES: No smoking
singing
dancing
shouting
swearing
fighting
cheating

SHOW RESPECT TO TEACHERS
ARRIVE NO LATER THAN 8:55
ALWAYS WRITE IN INK
SPEAK ONLY ENGLISH
SILENCE WHEN TEACHER IS TALKING
2 HOURS OF HOMEWORK EVERY NIGHT

Write more sentences about the "school rules" above, using these phrases:

We aren't allowed to …   *… isn't allowed.*   *They make us …*
They won't let us …   *We have to …*   *… is required.*

14.5   In other words …

Rewrite each sentence beginning with the words on the right.

1. I wish you wouldn't ask so many questions.   Please stop ....
2. NO PARKING ON SCHOOL GROUNDS   We aren't allowed ....
3. I get embarrassed when I meet strangers.   I'm not used ....
4. I didn't tell you my phone number.   I forgot ....
5. I feel sick if I eat too much ice cream.   .... too much ice cream ....

29

15 Prepositions – I

15.1 Mouse trouble

The Browns' house is full of mice. Explain exactly where each mouse is – but without pointing! Use the expressions below.

in front of
in the middle of
next to
beside
at the back of
on the edge of
in the corner of
on top of
below
underneath
behind
to the left of
to the right of
in between

15.2 In the mountains

Pair work   Fill in the blanks in this story.

There I was, standing alone .... the mountain looking .... the view. I could see the sun starting to set .... the west. Slowly a red glow spread .... the sky, until the sun finally went .... I could see gray clouds .... the sky and could feel a chill .... the air. Soon it would be very dark. I started to walk .... the slope .... the mountain hotel. I was going to spend the night .... I walked slowly, because the path was covered .... snow and ice. Suddenly it began to snow heavily. I stopped .... a tree and watched the flakes come .... I didn't want to get lost in the dark, so I walked on .... the snow.

   At last I saw the hotel .... me. By the time I reached it, I was very cold and wet. Once I was .... , however, I soon began to warm up. I sat .... the fire, drinking hot chocolate and singing songs .... my friends.

15.3 Where is my ... ?

Pair work   Take turns imagining that this desk belongs to you. It is so disorganized that you can never find what you need.

Student A: Ask your partner to help you find these things:
  coffee cup   pencil sharpener   calculator   address book   paper clips   cassette player

Student B: Ask your partner to help you find these things:
  scissors   box of airmail envelopes   pen   stapler   notebook   dictionary

15.4   Communication activity: Go straight until ...

Pair work   Student A should look at Activity 18, Student B at 45. You're going to describe a "route" to your partner.

You'll each need a pencil for this activity.

1	2	3	4	5	6	7	8	9	10
11	12	13	14	15	16	17	18	19	20
21	22	23	24	25	26	27	28	29	30
31	32	33	34	35	36	37	●	39	40
41	42	43	44	45	46	47	48	49	50
51	52	53	54	55	56	57	58	59	60
61	62	63	64	65	66	67	68	69	70
71	72	73	74	75	76	77	78	79	80
81	82	83	84	85	86	87	88	89	90
91	92	93	94	95	96	97	98	99	100

16 | *Prepositions – II*

16.1 This way, please!

A *Pair work*   Imagine that you are giving a tour of downtown Toronto. You want to show all the sights on this map. Work out the shortest possible route and mark it on the map.

B   Join another pair and explain your route to them. They should mark your route on the map as you tell them.

For example, you might begin talking about your route like this:

> *"First of all, we'll go out of Union Station and turn right. Then we'll walk along Front Street East until we get to the St. Lawrence Market, which will be on our right. From there we'll . . ."*

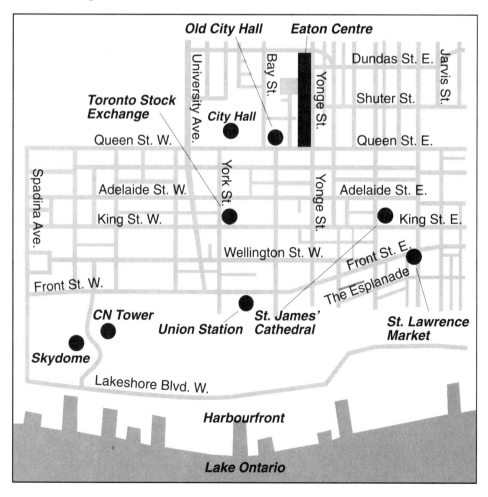

16.2 How do you feel?

A Which of these phrases go with the pictures below?

angry	furious	pleased		afraid	
annoyed	glad	sad	**+ about**	frightened	**+ of**
delighted	happy	thrilled		scared	
depressed	heart-broken	upset		terrified	
disappointed	nervous	worried			

She's ....
getting the job.

He's ....
tomorrow's exam.

She's ....
going out alone at night.

He's ....
being kept waiting.

She's ....
missing the show.

He's ....
leaving his girlfriend.

B *Pair work* Find out what kind of things your partner feels angry about, worried about, afraid of, etc.

16.3 Are you good at math?

A Put an appropriate preposition after each adjective and complete the sentences with your own ideas.

1. In school I used to be really good *at math and history.*
2. But I'm afraid I was pretty bad ....
3. Since graduating from school she has gotten very interested ....
4. He is very proud ....
5. Life in my country is quite different ....
6. Foreigners who visit my country are always impressed ....
7. By the time we arrived, the room was full ....
8. I always try to be polite ....
9. I didn't know you were studying. I'm sorry ......

B *Pair work* Write down the names of five outdoor sports, five indoor games, and five subjects you study (or studied) at school.

Then join another pair. Find out which of the things on your list they're interested in. Find out how good they are (or were) at them.

> I used to be more interested in .... than ....
> I'm not as interested in .... as ....

> I was better at .... than I was at ....
> I'm not as good at .... as I am at ....

17 *The future*

17.1 One day...

A *Pair work* Complete each sentence in your own words:

1. Tomorrow morning at 8:15, *I'll be having breakfast and reading the paper.*
2. One of these days, if I have enough money, I ....
3. By the time the bus .... , we'll all be soaking wet.
4. This weekend, if the weather's good, I ....
5. After this class is over, we ....
6. Their plane .... at 6:05 tomorrow morning.
7. As soon as I can, I ....
8. I .... tell anyone about our little secret.
9. Look out! That big black dog .... !
10. Since it's our teacher's birthday tomorrow, we ....

B Compare your sentences with another pair. See if they had the same ideas as you did.

C *Pair work* There is one error in each sentence. Find the errors and correct them.

1. I'll make some coffee when my friends will arrive.
2. I think I go out for a walk soon.
3. If they're going to have enough money, they're going abroad this summer.
4. We won't catch the train if we won't hurry.
5. Her sister-in-law has a baby next month.

34

17.2   Consequences

Group work   What would you reply to these statements?

1. *"I'm going to drink two whole liters of milk."*
2. *"I'm going to drive as fast as I can all the way there."*
3. *"I'm going to hold my breath for ten minutes."*
4. *"I'm not going to phone home this month."*
5. *"I'm going to steal that old woman's purse."*
6. *"I'm not going to come to this class ever again."*
7. *"I'm going to keep studying until my English is perfect."*

I'm going to go out in the rain.

But if you go out in the rain, you'll get wet!

17.3   Planning ahead

	MON	TUE	WED	THUR	FRI	SAT	SUN
a.m.							
p.m.							
evening							

A   Fill in your own plans and appointments for each day next week. You can add some imaginary plans too, if you like!

B   *Pair work*   Find out what your partner is going to do each day. Then find out how the plans might change if something *unexpected* happens.

For example: *"What will you do if you're sick on Monday morning?"*
 "What will you do if the weather's bad on Saturday afternoon?"

Some unexpected events might be:
  workers' strike   illness   bad weather   parents' visit   delay   accident

17.4   Next summer...

A   Fill in each blank with appropriate words or phrases:

Next summer I .... have a really great vacation. Of course, I .... have to save up for it and go without some luxuries, because otherwise I .... able to afford it. I haven't decided where I .... go yet. On the one hand it .... nice to go somewhere warm and sunny where I .... lie on the beach all day. On the other hand I .... get bored with that, so it .... better to choose a more active vacation. The important thing .... have a real change from routine. While I .... away, I .... send you a postcard!

B   *Group work*   Find out what your partners are going to do during their next vacation.

18 | *Possibility and probability*

18.1 Communication activity: Is it true?

A *Group work* Talk about the picture below, using these phrases:

Definitely	*It must be ...*		
Maybe	*It may be ...*	*It might be ...*	*It could be ...*
Maybe not	*It may not be ...*	*It might not be ...*	
Definitely not	*It can't be ...*		

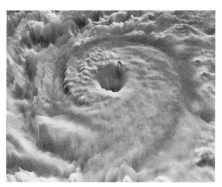

B Now Student A should look at Activity 6, Student B at 24, and C at 30.
You'll be discussing some information that may or may not be true.

18.2 How sure are you?

A Look at these examples.

Definitely	*I'm sure that it'll happen.*	*It's sure to happen.*
	It'll happen, that's for sure.	*It's going to happen.*
Probably	*It's likely to happen.*	*It may very well happen.*
	It'll probably happen.	*It might very well happen.*
Possibly	*It may happen.*	*It could happen.*
	It might happen.	
Possibly not	*It may not happen.*	*It might not happen.*
Probably not	*It's not likely to happen.*	*I don't think it'll happen.*
	It probably won't happen.	
Definitely not	*I'm sure that it won't happen.*	*It won't happen, that's for sure.*
	It couldn't happen.	*It's not going to happen.*

B *Pair work*   Write down your answers to these questions about the year 2050:

By the year 2050,
 will students in schools be taught by robots?
 will every home be controlled by computers?
 will there be a cure for every disease?
 will the climate be different? Will it be colder?
 will more world leaders be women?
 will people be living on Mars? Will you go there?
 will there be new kinds of transportation? What will they be?

For example: *I think it's unlikely that students will be taught by robots.*

C   Discuss your ideas with another pair. Do you share the same opinions?

D *Group work*   Talk about what is likely to happen to each of you in the future. How sure are you about what may happen during your lives…

 Six months from now …   One year from now …   In two years …
 In five years …   In ten years …   Eventually …

18.3   **What might have happened?**

A *Pair work*   Decide what might have happened in each of these scenes. For example:
 He might / could have been run over.   He could have had a skiing accident.

Then decide what is likely to happen next. For example:
 He'll probably have to stay in the hospital for a long time.

B   Write ten sentences about the pictures.

19 | *Verbs + prepositions*

19.1 Add the prepositions

A   Fill the blanks in these sentences with suitable prepositions.

1. I've looked everywhere .... my keys.
2. Who's going to look .... the business while you're away?
3. She tends to feel embarrassed when people look .... her.
4. Don't you know it's rude to stare .... people?
5. I'll never forgive them .... what they said to me.
6. I think you should apologize .... what you have done.

7. He threw the ball .... his friend, who caught it easily.
8. They were so mad they started throwing plates .... each other.
9. Afterwards they were able to laugh .... the incident.
10. We asked .... the check after our meal.
11. Don't laugh .... her or she'll get angry.
12. He gets very upset if someone shouts .... him.

13. Those plaid pants don't go .... your striped shirt.
14. I don't have my dictionary because I lent it .... a friend.
15. They borrowed $8,000 .... the bank to buy a new car.
16. How much did you pay .... the meal?
17. Thank you very much .... helping me.
18. Welcome .... Puerto Rico! I hope you enjoy your stay.

19. I'd like to speak .... you .... your work.
20. He didn't say anything .... me .... his plans.
21. I disagreed .... him .... what he should do.
22. She talked .... him .... the book she'd read.
23. He argued .... her .... her point of view.
24. I'm going to discuss it .... them tomorrow.

25. I dreamed .... prehistoric monsters last night.
26. What part of Canada do you come ....?
27. She's thinking .... changing her job soon.
28. I was just thinking .... how to solve this problem.
29. I was hungry, so she shared her sandwiches .... me.
30. We were all looking forward .... having dinner together.

B   Write your own examples for the *ten* verbs + prepositions you found hardest to remember. Compare your sentences with a partner.

19.2 Rearrange the sentences

Pair work   Match the beginnings and ends of these sentences, *and* add
the missing prepositions.

1. Everyone praised him ..*for*....   .... her own stupidity.
2. This house reminds me .... their favorite movie star.
3. We congratulated her .... telling lies and cheating on the exam.
4. I can't forgive him ....*1*.... doing so well on the exam.
5. She tried to blame us .... her performance in the concert.
6. They named their daughter .... a place I used to visit.
7. He punished his son .... being so rude to me.

19.3 Fill in the blanks

Fill in the blanks with an appropriate preposition.

1. It's hard for me to get used ....*to*.... foreign food.
2. It was easy to see .... his disguise.
3. Young Billy takes .... his father, Bill.
4. Maria looks .... her mother, doesn't she?
5. I don't feel .... going out for lunch today.
6. She's working .... a new book about James Dean.
7. Those yellow shoes don't go .... your green pants.
8. Driving after you've been drinking is asking .... trouble.
9. They spent a week in the capital and then headed .... the country.
10. The University of Hawaii sounds .... a good school. I'm going to send .... some
    information.
11. The letters TOEFL stand .... Test of English as a Foreign Language.

19.4 Use your own ideas...

A *Pair work*   Put an appropriate preposition after the verb in each
sentence. Then use your own ideas to complete each sentence.

1. I broke her glasses and she made me pay ..*for*.. ..*a new pair.*......
2. I'm excited because I'm going to play ..*in*.. ..*a tennis tournament.*..
3. He wasn't paying attention and crashed ....
4. I have to stay home tonight and prepare ....
5. All the furniture in the room belongs ....
6. Whether or not we go out depends ....
7. There was so much noise that I couldn't concentrate ....
8. In my opinion, an ideal breakfast consists ....
9. It was an awful hotel and we complained ....
10. We only had one sandwich, so it was divided ....

B   Show your completed sentences to another pair and compare your ideas.

C   Write your own examples for *ten* of the verbs + prepositions on this page
that you found hard to remember. Compare your sentences with a partner.

20 Phrasal verbs

20.1 We couldn't get down

A   Look at the words below. The verbs on the left can be used with most of the words on the right to form phrasal verbs (two words).

bring	fall	push
carry	get	ride
climb	go	run
come	jump	take
drive	pull	walk

around	in	past
away	off	up
back	on	
by	out	
down	over	

B   Add an appropriate phrasal verb to each of these sentences:

1. We climbed onto the camel, but then we couldn't ..*get*.. *down/off.*
2. If you don't want me to stay here, I'll ...*go*..... *away.*
3. She was standing in my way and I couldn't ....
4. The fence was too high for them to ....
5. When you've finished with my books please .... them ....
6. I realized that I was lost and was .... in circles.
7. His finger was stuck in the bottle and he couldn't .... it ....
8. Please .... your muddy boots before you come inside.

20.2 Word order

He wrote down the address. ✔   She ran down the hill. ✔
He wrote the address down. ✔   ~~She ran the hill down.~~
He wrote it down. ✔   ~~She ran it down.~~
~~He wrote down it.~~   She ran down it. ✔

In each of the following pairs of sentences, one is correct and the other is incorrect. Cross out the incorrect sentences.

1. ~~He jumped the cliff off.~~   He jumped off the cliff.
2. They opened up them.   They opened up their presents.
3. It's hard work bringing up children.   It's hard work bringing up them.
4. The car drove the bridge over.   The car drove over the bridge.
5. She walked it past.   She walked past it.
6. I'm working on my science project.   I'm working it on.
7. He took off his coat.   He took off it.
8. Your socks don't go with those pants.   Your socks don't go them with.
9. Flowers come out in the spring.   Flowers come in the spring out.

20.3 In other words...

Select one phrasal verb from the lists beside the sentences to replace a word or phrase in each sentence.

1. The plane left on time. *The plane took off on time.*
2. We began our trip early in the morning.
3. We intended to interrupt our trip in Honolulu.
4. There was a thunderstorm but the plane continued flying.
5. But soon the pilot decided to return to Tokyo.

stop off / over
take off
turn back
start out
keep on

break down
check in
check out
get together
wear out

6. When I finally arrived at the hotel I registered.
7. The elevator was old and beyond repair.
8. It usually stopped working after breakfast.
9. I called a friend of mine, and we arranged to meet for a meal.
10. At the end of my stay I paid my bill and left the hotel.

11. Whenever there are games at parties I like to participate.
12. During the party all the lights stopped working.
13. We continued playing our game in the dark.
14. Suddenly there was a bang like a bomb exploding.
15. Then all the lights started working again.

go out
join in
go off
go on
keep on

20.4 Fill in the blanks

Use one phrasal verb from the lists beside the sentences to replace a word or phrase in each sentence. In some cases you'll have to add a pronoun.

leave on
turn up
turn down
turn on
turn off

1. Let's listen to some music on the radio. Can you ...*turn it on, please?*...........
2. That's way too loud. Please ......
3. Oh, the news is on. Could you ...... now, please?
4. Gee, the news is so depressing, I'd like you to ......
5. But if *you* want to hear it, go ahead and ......

6. Last year I ...... my job of 10 years.
7. I don't know what ...... this change of heart.
8. It wasn't easy to ...... the topic of quitting with my boss.
9. The company had to hire someone else to ...... my duties.
10. I ...... all my possessions so I could travel.

carry out
bring up
give away
give up
bring on

call back
call off
call up
put off
put through

11. I wanted to ...... my meeting with Mr. Brown.
12. So I ...... first thing in the morning.
13. I had to wait while the operator tried to ......
14. His secretary said he was busy and asked me to ......
15. I said no, and threatened to ...... the whole deal.

16. I have this very complicated form to ......
17. I've written the wrong date, so I'd better ......
18. I can't ...... this word – the type is too faint.
19. I don't know my grandmother's maiden name, so I'll just ...
20. I've had enough of this: Could you please ...... ?

take away
make up
fill out
cross out
make out

21 *If ... sentences – I*

21.1 *If, unless, when, until*

> *Take one tablet every hour if you're in pain. Don't take one unless you need it. Stop taking them when the pain goes away.*

Use *if*, *unless*, *when*, or *until* in these sentences. In some cases there are several possibilities.

1. The radio won't work ...*unless/until*... you put some batteries in.
2. I can't work .... you keep interrupting.
3. Come and see me .... you feel lonely.
4. We'll have coffee .... we've finished.
5. Let's wait .... our friends arrive.
6. I'll call you .... I get to the airport.
7. You can't do that .... you have permission.
8. We'll go by car .... you want to walk.
9. Don't phone me .... you need my help.

21.2 What are you going to do?

Pair work   Imagine that you have various plans for tomorrow, but your plans depend on the weather and other circumstances. Follow the pattern below to talk about your intentions.

> *I might go hiking if the weather's nice.*

> *And what if it isn't nice?*

> *Well, I'm certainly not going hiking unless the weather is nice!*

ACTIVITY	DEPENDS ON
hike	weather being good
shopping	having enough money
concert	getting tickets
zoo	friends wanting to go
swimming	water being warm
dinner	finding a good restaurant
movies	something good playing
study	being in the mood

21.3 If, if, if...

Look at these examples, then fill in the blanks on the next page.

IF I PASS THE EXAM, I'LL GO OUT AND CELEBRATE!

IF I KNEW MORE, I'D BE SURE TO PASS!

IF I HADN'T WASTED SO MUCH TIME, I'D HAVE LEARNED MORE!

1. If you ....*drive*........ carefully, you ......*won't have*........ an accident.
2. If he .... a better driver, he .... have so many accidents.
3. If she .... more carefully last night, she .... an accident.
4. If the weather .... this weekend, we .... have a picnic.
5. If I .... President, I ....

21.4 Just suppose...

Group work   Ask each other these questions:

How would your life be different if you were much...
  younger   taller   more intelligent   more patient
  older   shorter   less intelligent   less patient ?

Or if you were... *famous   very rich   a movie star   a different nationality ?*

21.5 First prize!

Group work   Imagine that you have entered a contest. You are
dreaming about the prizes.

Which prizes would you choose to have instead of taking the money?
If you took the cash, what would you spend it on?

1st PRIZE	2nd PRIZE	3rd PRIZE	4h PRIZE	5th PRIZE
$100,000 in cash!!! or **a luxury villa in the Caribbean!!!** or **$5,000 worth of groceries a year for the rest of your life!!!**	**$20,000 in cash!!** or **a Toyota Camry!!** or **TWO Volkswagen Rabbits!!**	**$2,000 in cash!** or **an Apple Macintosh computer!** or **a Technics stereo system!**	**$500 in cash!** or **a Sony color TV** or **a Panasonic video recorder**	**$100 in cash!** or **a set of matching suitcases** or **a copy of this book personally signed by The Author**

21.6 Complete the sentences

Pair work   Complete these sentences, using your own ideas.

1. If I get up late tomorrow, ...
2. If it snows a lot this winter, ...
3. If I lived in China, ...
4. If I have a headache tomorrow, ...
5. If I were a nicer person, ...
6. Unless you leave immediately, ...

7. I won't come and see you if ....
8. I wouldn't be very happy if ....
9. I'll take a message if ....
10. I'm not going out tonight unless ....
11. I would speak better English if ....
12. The world would be a better place if ....

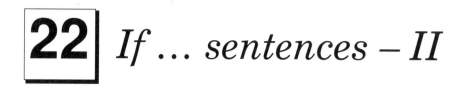

22.1   She didn't win

Poor Mary! She was sure she was going to win, but she didn't. What could she have done if she had won?

Write five sentences beginning:

If Mary had won, …

22.2   What would you have done?

A   *Pair work*   Ask your partner these questions about the places in the list below:

What would you have done if you'd spent your last vacation in these countries?
What places could you have visited?   *What food might you have eaten?*

Brazil   Australia   Hawaii   Thailand
England   France   Italy   Japan
Korea   Spain   Taiwan

B   Join another pair and find out what *they* would have done in the same places. Would you have done the same things?

22.3   If I'd been there…

Pair work   Imagine what you might have seen or could have done if you'd been in the places listed on page 45 at the right time. Look at this example first:

IF I'D BEEN IN BELGIUM IN 1815, I MIGHT HAVE SEEN NAPOLEON DEFEATED AT WATERLOO.

Belgium   1815   Napoleon defeated at Waterloo

44

Vienna, Austria	1791	Mozart conducted premiere of *The Magic Flute*
London, England	1863	First underground railway opened
Paris, France	1895	First showing of a movie to the public
Kitty Hawk, North Carolina	1903	Orville Wright flew first successful airplane
Anaheim, California	1955	Disneyland opened
Cape Kennedy, Florida	1969	First manned rocket took off for the Moon
Seoul, South Korea	1988	24th Olympic Games
Berlin, Germany	1989	Berlin Wall opened

22.4   What if…?

Group work   Ask each other these questions. Encourage each other to be as imaginative as possible!

What if you'd been born a member of the opposite sex?
– How would your life have been different so far?
– What would have happened to you?
– What wouldn't have happened that has actually happened?
– How would your life be different now?

What if you'd been born …
  … in the United States?
  … the son or daughter of a millionaire?
  … with an ability to see the future?
  … a genius?

22.5   In other words…

Rewrite each sentence, beginning with *If* …

1. We stayed up all night, and that's why we're so tired this morning.
   If we hadn't stayed up all night, we wouldn't be so tired this morning.
2. He wasn't able to answer the questions, so he failed the exam.
3. I didn't see you there, or I'd have said hello.
4. The reason I haven't been to Hawaii is that I can't afford it.
5. They didn't go to the beach because the weather was so bad.
6. She hasn't studied English before – that's why she's in an introductory class.
7. One of the reasons I didn't phone you was that I was very busy.
8. They won the game because two of our players were injured.

22.6   Three paragraphs

Write three paragraphs, beginning as follows:
  If I had lots of money, …
  If the weather's nice this weekend, …
  If I'd worked harder at school, …

23 *The passive – I*

23.1 **It has to be redecorated!**

A   Before Maria and Brian can move into
their new apartment, it has to be redecorated.
Amy and Bob are doing the work for them.

Complete these sentences, using the passive.

1. They gave the job to Amy and Bob.   → Amy and Bob *were given the job.*
2. They started the work last week.   → The work *was started last week.*
3. They finished the kitchen on Monday.   → The kitchen ....
4. They were doing the bedroom on Friday.   → The bedroom ....
5. They're painting the living room now.   → The living room ....
6. They have painted the walls green.   → The walls ....
7. They're going to paint the ceiling pink.   → The ceiling ....
8. They will finish the work next week.   → The work ....

B   *Pair work*   Look at the decoration of the room you're in now. Talk
about what has been done and what needs to be done.

23.2 **Communication activity: Color blind?**

Pair work   Student A should look at Activity 19, while Student B looks
at 47. Imagine that your apartments were redecorated while you were on
vacation. Unfortunately, your instructions were not followed. Find out what
was done wrong in your partner's apartment.

23.3 **Spot the errors**

Pair work   Find the mistakes in each of these sentences and correct
them.

1. Romeo and Juliet were written from Shakespeare.
2. I can't give you a ride because my car is repairing.
3. I were told that, after been repaired, it will be as good as new.
4. It thought that many diseases caused by smoking cigarettes.
5. We were telling to arrive by noon, but we were delay.
6. It was announce for the company president that large profits had be made.

23.4 Communication activity: Has everything been done?

Pair work Student A should look at Activity 7, while Student B looks at 34. You'll be finding out what jobs have been done (or not done) at a garage and before a party.

Imagine that you're on the phone. Use the patterns shown in this picture.

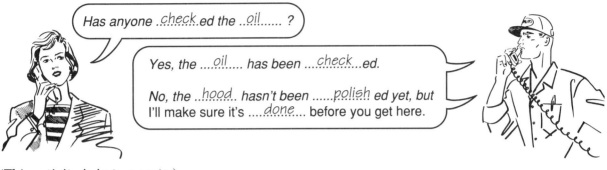

Has anyone ..*check*.ed the ..*oil*...... ?

Yes, the ....*oil*.... has been ...*check*...ed.

No, the ..*hood*.. hasn't been ......*polish* ed yet, but I'll make sure it's ....*done*... before you get here.

(This activity is in two parts.)

23.5 Giving instructions

A Rewrite these instructions, using simple commands instead of the passive.

A regular size sheet of typing paper (8 ½ x 11 inches or A4) needs to be used for this experiment. First of all, it has to be torn into four smaller pieces. This is done as follows:

1. It has to be folded in the middle and then it can be torn into two pieces.

2. Each piece is folded again across the middle and torn to make a total of four equal-size pieces.

Now one of the pieces is placed on the table with the long sides pointing down. A horizontal line is drawn across the top of the paper about a quarter of the way from the top. Then two vertical lines are drawn downwards from the horizontal line, so that the bottom part of the paper is divided into three equal-size parts.

Next, the paper has to be torn along each of these vertical lines as far as the horizontal line so that three flaps are created. Then the left flap is folded toward you and the right flap is folded away from you – the folds are made right at the top of the flap. The center flap should not be not folded, though.

Now a paper clip has to be found and this is attached to the bottom of the center flap. Finally, the whole thing has to be raised high and is then allowed to fall …

Begin like this:

Use a regular-size sheet of typing paper (8 ½ x 11 inches or A4) for this experiment. First of all, tear it into four smaller pieces. Do this as follows: …

B Carry out the experiment, following the instructions you have written.

C *Group work* Explain to your partners how another object can be made using the three pieces of paper you didn't use in part B.

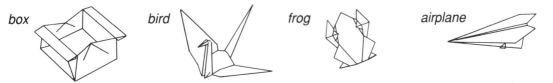

box   bird   frog   airplane

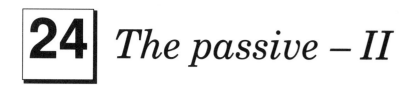

24 *The passive – II*

24.1 Who by?

Group work   Match the two columns. Then make a sentence for each,
using the passive. Look at the example on the right first.

> *I think penicillin was discovered by Alexander Fleming.*

1. *Guernica*   .... Margaret Mitchell
2. Radium   .... Picasso
3. Penicillin   .... Agatha Christie
4. *Rashomon*   .... Thomas Edison
5. Light bulbs   .... Madonna
6. *Gone with the Wind*   .... Alexander Fleming
7. Walkman stereo   .... Walt Disney
8. Mickey Mouse   .... Cambridge University Press
9. "Material Girl"   .... Sony
10. *War and Peace*   .... Marie Curie
11. This book   .... Akira Kurosawa
12. *Murder on the Orient Express*   .... Leo Tolstoy

24.2 News headlines

Rewrite these newspaper headlines as complete sentences, using the passive.

Theft of valuable painting from National Gallery

A valuable painting has been stolen from the National Gallery.

Over 100 highway deaths last month

Over 24,000 new businesses begun last year

Spacecraft discovers new planet beyond Pluto

15 students arrested after demonstration

Mexico wins soccer championship

Manager accused of accepting bribes — forced to resign

Missing airliner found in jungle — survivors rescued by helicopter

24.3 Communication activity: Being...

Pair work Student A should look at Activity 38, while Student B looks at 42. Use the expressions below to react to each other's promises, threats, and offers.

Oh no! I don't like .....*being criticized.*.....

How awful! I hate ....
I can't stand ....

.....*Being criticized.*..... is awful.

.... is upsetting.
.... isn't much fun.

I don't want to .....*to be criticized.*.....

I wouldn't like to ....
It's awful to ....

Great! I like ....
Wonderful! I love ....
How nice! I enjoy ....

Being .... is nice.
.... is great.
.... is fun.

I'd like to be ....
It's nice to be ....
It's fun to be ....

24.4 Passive ➛ Active ➛ Passive

A Look at the example and then rewrite each sentence.

1. The plants got damaged by the cold weather.
   The cold weather damaged the plants.

2. Steven got punished by his father.
3. Ann's leg got broken in a skiing accident.
4. Dozens of trees got blown down by the wind.
5. Karen was awarded the prize by the judges.
6. The new airport is going to be opened by the mayor.
7. If you can't drive, who is your car going to be driven by?
8. Your birthday presents can't be opened until your birthday.

B Rewrite these sentences using the passive.

1. Someone has stolen my watch.
   My watch has been stolen.

2. The voters reelected the President.
3. The police are interviewing all the witnesses.
4. We're going to give David a big surprise!
5. The maid hasn't cleaned my hotel room.
6. Someone has asked me to give a talk about my country.
7. The people at the garage have to fix my car before I can drive it.
8. They're showing that movie you wanted to see this week.

25 | *Prepositional phrases – I*

25.1 In...

in bed   prison   jail   church   school
a store   the hospital   the park
pencil   ink   pen   ballpoint
the snow   the rain   the sun   the cold   the fog
the air   the sky   the country
the evening   the daytime   the morning   the afternoon
private   public   silence   secret
a loud voice   a soft voice   a whisper   a deep voice   a kind voice
a good mood   a terrible mood   good spirits
danger   trouble   love   pain   tears   debt   a hurry
sight   pieces   reach   store   flames   stock   luck
Montreal   Japan   Sue's room   my apartment
five minutes   half an hour   a moment   a little while   ten days
a red hat   a green sweater   a dirty raincoat   his pajamas   bare feet

Pair work   Complete each sentence in at least *two* ways, using the
phrases above:

1. Everyone laughed when he came to school ...*in his pajamas/in his bare feet.*..
2. I'd rather be .... than ....
3. It's boring here indoors – let's go out ....
4. I usually read the newspaper ....
5. Poor Sam! He had to spend three weeks ....
6. She smiled sympathetically and then spoke to me ....
7. He's having a rough time and he's often ....
8. You can see from her expression that she's ....
9. Such an important meeting should be held ....
10. On an exam it's best to write your answers ....

25.2 Going...

by car bus taxi train plane sea ship
bike subway
in a bus a car a taxi a train
an elevator the bus the car the taxi
the train the elevator

for a walk a drive a ride a run a swim
on a train a ship a bus a bike a plane
a subway the train the bus the subway
a trip a cruise a tour an outing foot

Examples: *They went for a drive in the car.   I traveled to Australia by plane.*

50

Pair work   Ask each other these questions. Use the phrases on page 50 to answer them:

– How exactly did you get to school today?
– What did you do last weekend?
– What did you do on your last vacation?
– How would you get from the place you're sitting now all the way to the top of the Empire State Building in New York?
– What's your favorite way of traveling? Why do you prefer it?

25.3   By heart

by	*on*	*at*	*out of*
heart	vacation	home	date
accident	purpose	school	sight
mistake	business	college	danger
day	duty	work	work
night	strike	the movies	the question
myself	my own	first	control
the way	fire	once	reach
all means	sale	the beginning	stock
telephone	the telephone	sea	order
letter	the radio	last	luck
fax	a diet	least	breath
		night	his/her mind
		the end	time

off duty   *up to* date   *under* control

Pair work   Use the phrases in the lists above to complete each of the following sentences in an interesting way:

1. "Hello, I'm calling the Fire Department because *..this fire is getting out of control.....................*"
2. We can't go to school today because.....
3. The news must be true because.....
4. I refuse to do any work at all because.....
5. You can't punish them because.....
6. No one likes him because.....
7. I'm not supposed to eat chocolate because.....
8. They weren't allowed to enter the country because.....
9. The only way to remember these phrases is......

25.4   Finally…

A   Look back through the phrases in this unit and choose *ten* phrases that were difficult to remember. Write them in your notebook, and then compose a sentence using each phrase.

B   *Pair work*   Compare your sentences with your partner's.

26 Prepositional phrases – II

26.1 Time flies!

They arrived... **on time   in time   in plenty of time**
just in time   in the nick of time
at the same time

That was **before my time**.   He's **behind the times**.
She feels tired **at times**.   She gets angry **from time to time**.
He's in a bad mood **all the time**.   It was finished **in no time at all**.

Pair work   Use the phrases above to complete each of these sentences in
your own words.

1. These clothes are old-fashioned and ...*behind the times*...
2. If you go by plane.....   5. The twins.....
3. The lifeboat.....   6. I finished the exam.....
4. Everyone should.....   7. If you're going to an interview.....

26.2 In time for...

in addition to	in charge of	in front of	in love with	at the point of
in answer to	in comparison with	with the help of	by means of	in search of
at the beginning of	in control of	in honor of	in the mood for	at the start of
on behalf of	at the end of	in the hope of	at peace with	in time for
				at war with

Complete these sentences, using the the phrases above:

1. The assistant manager signed the report .....*on behalf of*..... Ms. Brown.
2. Ms. Brown is the person who is .... this department.
3. My brother says that he's .... the girl next door!
4. We're having a big party .... our parents' 50th wedding anniversary.
5. The sales manager went to the conference .... getting new customers.
6. The audience started clapping and cheering .... the show.
7. I couldn't see the stage because the person .... me was so tall.
8. I think I'll go out for a walk because I'm not .... studying.
9. The magician lifted the table .... his two assistants.
10. The two countries are still .... each other after all this time.
11. .... your question – I have no idea what the answer is.
12. They went up the Amazon in 1925 .... El Dorado.
13. I know it's late, but am I still .... dinner?

26.3   On the one hand...

on the one hand ... on the other hand   *for example*   *for instance*
in other words   *in general*
in fact   *as a matter of fact*   *on the whole*
in any case   *at any rate*   *at least* *in the long run*
according to her   *in theory*
in his opinion   *in practice*

Use the phrases above in these sentences:

1. I've thought about your proposals. Although *on the one hand* our profits will probably increase, ... we'll all have to work harder.
2. She seemed to be asleep – .... her eyes were shut.
3. Ruth has some strange ideas: .... , men are inferior to women!
4. I see what you mean and .... I agree with you, but I don't think your ideas will work ....
5. There are several things I don't understand: .... why do I need a visa to enter the United States?
6. I sometimes have problems with reading a map – .... I usually get lost when I'm using one.
7. I know it's a big expense right now, but .... it will end up saving you money.

26.4   A little walk

Fill in each blank in the story below with one or more words. Use the words you have learned in this unit and the previous one.

The weather was so nice ......*in*........ the afternoon that I decided to go .... a little walk .... my new boots – the ones I'd seen advertised .... TV as "the World's Best Boots." Well, ... theory, they were very comfortable boots, but I soon realized that .... fact they gave me blisters. Now, ... I enjoy walking, but by now I was .... such pain that I was .... a really bad mood. All I wanted was rest and refreshment. .... , I wanted to sit down, have a drink, and return home .... bus. The last bus home was .... half an hour, so I had to get to the nearest bus stop .... a hurry. .... last, the bus stop was .... sight! I limped to the bus stop .... the hope .... getting on, but I was .... luck. The bus was completely full – not even standing room! I knew I'd never make it home .... foot. I was .... the point .... giving up hope when another bus arrived, completely empty! I got on and sat down .... the back. I began to feel .... peace .... the world again as I took off my boots!

26.5   Finally...

Look back through the phrases in this unit and choose *ten* phrases that were difficult to remember. Write them in your notebook, and then compose a sentence using each phrase. Compare your sentences with a partner's.

27 | *Reported speech: statements*

27.1 What do you think?

She says that ...   She thinks that ...
According to her ...   She believes that ...
Apparently ...   She feels that ...

A Ask at least three other students for their opinions on the topics below.
Make notes to help you remember what they say.

Not wearing a seat belt   Wearing jeans to work   Watching 30 hours of TV per week
Cheating on an exam   Breaking the speed limit   Not returning a borrowed book
Smoking in public places   Getting up in the afternoon Eating ice cream for breakfast
Not paying your taxes   Going to bed at 3 a.m.   Borrowing money from friends

B *Pair work* Now find a partner and report what you found out.

27.2 What did they say?

She told me that ...   He replied that ...   He added that ...
She announced that ...   He answered that ...   He admitted that ...
She complained that ...   He explained that ...   He suggested that ...

Use the reporting verbs above to report what Jim said on the next page.

*Hi, Sandy. Wasn't that an awful storm last
    night?*
I don't like thunderstorms.
I get nervous if there's a thunderstorm.
The sky's very cloudy today.
It'll probably rain later on.
*I'm going to take my new umbrella to work
    with me.*
I just bought it yesterday.
Maybe I can use it for the first time.
I haven't had a chance to try it out yet.
I won't mind if it rains today.
*But I hope there won't be any thunder or
    lightning.*
If I hear any thunder, I'll stay indoors.
I guess I'm a coward, aren't I?

I was talking to Jim earlier and ...

*He told me that he didn't like thunderstorms.
He admitted ...*

27.3   Communication activity: Guess what!

Pair work   Student A should look at Activity 32, Student B at 40. You're
going to be telling your partner about a conversation you had the other day.
Begin like this:

A: *Mary told me that she and John had been married for eight years.*
B: *That's funny, because John told me that he had only known Mary for six
   years. He said they had first met at a New Year's Eve party.*

27.4   In other words...

Change the dialogue below into reported speech.

Ann: You really must do something about your hair, Tom.
Tom: But I like having long hair.
Ann: Well, I think it looks ridiculous like that.
Tom: No it doesn't. And it's the latest style.
Ann: Huh! Long hair on men hasn't been in style for years.
Tom: I don't care. What matters is whether I look good or not.
Ann: But you look awful, especially now that you're starting to go bald.
Tom: I am *not* going bald! I just don't have as much hair as I used to.
Ann: You're just afraid to go to the barber in case he laughs.
Tom: Well, it's true I haven't been to a barber in ages, but...
Ann: I have an idea! I'll cut it for you myself. Sit down here.
Tom: I don't trust you. You'll cut it so short that everyone will think
      I've just come out of the army!
Ann: I'll just get some scissors...

Example: *Ann told Tom that he had to do something about his hair.*

28.1 What did he want to know?

He asked (me) if …   *He tried to find out if …*
He wondered if …   *He asked (me) why …*
He wanted to know if …   *He wanted to know when …*

Imagine that you decided to pay a surprise visit to some friends last week.
Report the questions that your friends asked you, using the phrases above.

> *Well hello! Welcome!*
> *Did you have a good trip?*
> *When did you arrive?*
> *Have you had lunch yet?*
> *Would you like something to drink?*
> *Did you have any trouble finding our house?*
> *Why didn't you phone us?*
> *How long are you going to stay?*
> *Will you be able to stay till the weekend?*
> *Do you mind sleeping on the sofa?*
> *Why didn't you bring your sleeping bag?*

> *They welcomed me.*
> *They wondered if I'd had a good trip.*
> *They asked me when I'd arrived.*
> *They wanted …*

28.2 A very good day

A Think about some of the places you've been to and things you've done
recently. Try to think of one day that was especially fun or memorable. What
made that day special?

B *Pair work* Ask about your partner's special day. Find out:
– what happened that day and what made it special
– what might have made it even more enjoyable
– how that special day was different from more "normal" days.

C Write a report of your partner's day in one or two paragraphs.
Begin like this: *My partner told me …*

28.3 What did he ask you?

A *Pair work* Ask your partner ten questions – about anything you like.

B Now change partners. Find out what questions your new partner was asked earlier. Maybe start like this:

You: *What did he ask you?*
Your partner: *He asked me where I was born.*
You: *Oh really? My partner asked me where I was born, too. What
                   else did he ask you?*

28.4 What did she want you to do?

She asked me to …   *She advised me to …*   *She warned me (not) to …*
She told me to …   *She tried to persuade me to …*   *She invited me to …*
She wanted me to …   *She encouraged me to …*   *She reminded me to …*
She ordered me to …   *She urged me to …*

Imagine that an old friend is talking to you on the phone. Use the verbs above
to report these things she said to you:

> *You sound tired – try to relax more.*
> *If I were you I wouldn't work so hard.*
> *You'll feel better if you get some fresh air.*
> *Why don't you go out for a walk?*
> *Don't spend so much time studying.*
> *You really must come and see us soon.*
> *Listen, would you like to have dinner on Monday?*
> *Please come – we haven't seen you for ages.*
> *Please get here before 7:30.*
> *And don't forget to bring some dessert!*
> *You'd better write down my address.*
> *And call me if you get lost on the way.*

> *She told me to relax more.*
> *She advised me not to …*

28.5 Communication activity: In other words …

A *Group work* Half of each group
should look at Activity 29, while the other half
looks at Activity 37. There are two different
versions of the same conversation, which you
will have to rewrite in dialogue form.

B When you have finished rewriting the
conversations, show your version to the other
half of your group. What are the differences?
What do you think was *really* said?

29 Relative clauses

29.1 This is the man who...

How do you think this
conversation might continue?

29.2 Communication activity: What's her name?

Pair work   Student A should look at Activity 14, Student B at 25. Talk
about the women above, following this pattern:

B: What's the name of the woman **who**'s wearing glasses?
A: Her name's Kumiko.
B: Oh, really? She's the woman (**who/that**) I met in Tokyo two years ago.

29.3 Communication activity: What's it about?

Group work   Student A should look at Activity 22, Student B at 36,
and Student C at 44. You're going to tell each other what the following books,
plays, movies, or stories are about. Follow this pattern:

A: Does anyone know what *Hamlet* is about?
B: Yes, it's about a prince **who** wants to kill his father's murderer.

Hamlet   *Don Quixote*   *Cats*   *Batman*   *Kramer versus Kramer*   *Superman*
E.T.   *King Kong*   *Gone with the Wind*   *One Hundred Years of Solitude*
Dallas   *Sherlock Holmes*   *Tampopo*   *Frankenstein*   *Romeo and Juliet*

29.4 My friend John, whose …

Use *who*, *whose*, *where*, *when*, *that*, or *which* to complete each sentence. Be careful about where you put the commas!

John Smith, whose photo is in the paper, is an old friend of mine.

The woman whose photo is in the paper looks like an old friend of mine.

1. The place ....*where*...... I went to school is a quiet town.   *(no commas)*
2. Montreal**,** ....*where*...... I went to college**,** is a beautiful city.
3. My oldest brother .... has a moustache is studying architecture.
4. The man .... I saw on television is a famous writer.
5. The day .... we left on our trip was Friday the 13th.
6. The time .... I broke my leg skiing is one of my worst memories.
7. The car .... was stolen was a blue Toyota.
8. My car .... I've had since 1989 is a white Honda.
9. The airline .... I took to Hong Kong had wonderful service.
10. The Hotel Tyrol .... I stayed when I was in Italy was a really nice hotel.

29.5 Connections

Use *who* or *which* to make single sentences.

1. I called to Luis. He saw me. He waved at me.

   I called to Luis, who waved at me when he saw me.

2. Mary ate four ice cream cones. They made her feel sick.
3. I'm going to the mountains for my vacation. I'm really looking forward to this.
4. I went to see a movie. It was about space monsters. It gave me nightmares.
5. We started talking to Kim. She told us about her adventures in the jungle.
6. I wrote them an angry letter. This made me feel much calmer afterwards.
7. I spent a long time with Tom. He was very helpful. He gave me some good advice.
8. You'd better rewrite this letter. You wrote it too quickly and carelessly.

29.6 In other words …

Rewrite each sentence, beginning with the words on the right.

1. I started work on January 2nd.   The day *I started work was January 2nd.*
2. She was wearing old and dirty clothes.   The clothes …
3. I was given the message by someone wearing a brown jacket.   The person …
4. My favorite film is *Casablanca*, made in 1942.   *Casablanca* …
5. An old school friend gave me a job.   The person …
6. You were rude to that woman's husband, and she's upset now.   The woman …
7. I bought a computer on sale and it doesn't work.   The computer …
8. My cousin Pete helped me study for my history exam.   Pete …

30 Joining sentences – I

30.1 When...

I was eating my lunch when John came in.

I ate my lunch when John came in.

I had already eaten my lunch when John came in.

Pair work   Use your own words to complete each sentence in this story:

1. When he heard the phone ringing, ...
2. When he got to the phone, ...
3. When it rang again, ...
4. When he heard his fiancée's voice, ...
5. When she told him the news, ...
6. When he had recovered from his shock, ...
7. When he hung up, ...
8. When the phone rang again later, ...
9. When we saw him the next morning, ...

30.2 Rearrange the sentences

Match the two halves of each sentence.

1. I held my breath
2. I didn't leave the room
3. I bought a new coat
4. I used to get in trouble
5. I forgot to wash my hands
6. I sent the package
7. I had eaten all her candy
8. I went on vacation
9. I waited patiently
10. I was able to do the exercise

.... until I had finished all my work.
.... when I'd saved up enough money.
...*1*.... as the door opened slowly.
.... by the time she came back.
.... until they arrived.
.... whenever I came home late.
.... soon after the weather turned cold.
.... before I had dinner.
.... as soon as I found the address.
.... once I'd found the answers in the back.

60

30.3 Join the sentences

Make one sentence from each pair of sentences, using *While ...*, *After ...*,
Before ..., or *When ....*

1. I paid $200 for a suit. Later I saw the same one at half the price.
    After I paid $200 for a suit, I saw the same one at half the price.
2. I reported my passport missing. Afterwards I found it in my suitcase.
3. They entered the house. Then they took off their hats and coats.
4. She was in college. During that time she made a lot of new friends.
5. He told me he was your brother. Until then I had no idea who he was.
6. I got a lot of work done. Before that I took the phone off the hook.
7. You're going to leave the house. Before that, make sure you lock the door.
8. You're going to finish this exercise. Afterwards, you can have a short rest.

30.4 Just in case

in case
because
although   *even though*
so that
if   *as long as*   *provided that*
unless

I'm wearing sunglasses . . .
in case the sun shines later.
because the sun may shine.
even though it's not sunny now.

Work in pairs. Decide which of the words above you can use to complete these
sentences:

1. She brought an umbrella ..... *in case* ..... it rains later.
2. He's wearing a hat .... he doesn't want people to know he's bald.
3. I didn't go to bed .... I had an awful cold and a fever.
4. I'm going to study hard .... I'll pass the exam.
5. You can teach me to drive .... you promise not to get mad at me.
6. I won't speak to her again .... she apologizes.
7. I'm going dancing tonight .... my ankle is swollen.
8. The town was flooded .... it had rained so heavily.
9. We're going out for a walk .... the weather stays nice.
10. I'm going to take some sandwiches .... I get hungry.

30.5 In other words...

Rewrite each sentence so that it has the same meaning.

1. We went swimming in spite of the rain.   Although ....
    Although it was raining, we went swimming.
2. The trains were late due to bad weather.   Because the weather ....
3. He broke the teapot because of his clumsiness.   Because ....
4. They passed the test in spite of their laziness.   Even though ....
5. She left early in order to catch her train.   She left early so that ....
6. She missed the train despite leaving early.   Although ....

31 Joining sentences – II

31.1 Both ... and ...

	Ann	Tom	Sue	Bill
meat	✓	✓	✗	✗
fish	✓	✗	✗	✓
rice	✗	✗	✗	✓
potatoes	✓	✗	✓	✗
pasta	✓	✓	✓	✓
eggs	✓	✓	✗	✓
bananas	✗	✓	✓	✗

Both Ann and Tom like meat.
Neither Sue nor Bill likes meat.

Sue dislikes both meat and fish.
Sue doesn't like either meat or fish.
Sue likes neither meat nor fish.

Only Bill likes rice.
None of them likes rice except Bill.
Everyone except Sue likes eggs.

A   Make up more sentences like these about the people in the chart.

B   *Group work*   Find out about the likes and dislikes of the people in your group. Make a similar chart.

C   Write sentences about the people in your group. Use the structures above.

31.2   Communication activity: Uncles!

Pair work   Student A should look at Activity 41, while Student B looks at 46. You're going to describe some uncles!

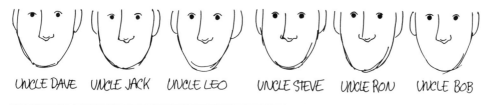

UNCLE DAVE   UNCLE JACK   UNCLE LEO   UNCLE STEVE   UNCLE RON   UNCLE BOB

31.3   Fog at the airport

Combine each pair of sentences to make one longer sentence.

1. There was fog at the airport.   This had caused all flights to be delayed.
   All flights were delayed because of fog at the airport.   or
   All flights were delayed because there was fog at the airport.
2. Amy and Paul were waiting for the same flight.   As a result they started talking.
3. She was feeling very hungry.   The reason was that she hadn't had any breakfast.
4. He offered her a sandwich.   She was so hungry that she accepted the offer.

5. They both liked music.   That was why they got along well.
6. He enjoyed playing the piano.   And so did she.
7. He was much older than she.   Nevertheless, she found him very attractive.
8. They had a big fight the next day.   Still, they decided to get married.
9. She enjoyed his cooking.   Moreover, she enjoyed his company too.
10. He never let her go out alone.   This was to prevent her from meeting other men.

31.4 Solving problems

However... Nevertheless... But...
That's why... Therefore... So...
Otherwise...
Meanwhile...
Unfortunately... Luckily... Fortunately...
Believe it or not... Strangely enough...
In fact... Actually...
In other words... That is to say...

Pair work   Decide which words you can use to connect these pairs of
sentences.

1. You can go by plane.   .... if that scares you, you can take the train.
2. I thought the plane would be delayed.   .... I brought a book to read.
3. Everyone in my class got sick with the flu.   .... I was the only one who didn't get it!
4. I discovered I didn't have any cash with me.   .... I had my credit card.
5. I knew it was likely to rain.   .... we decided to have a picnic.
6. I just spent my last dollar.   .... I'm flat broke.
7. Remember to take your passport.   .... you won't be allowed to cross the border.
8. They fell into the ocean.   .... neither of them could swim.

31.5 Communication activity: The reasons why...

1   In the first place...
   To begin with...
   First of all...
   One reason...

2   In the second place...   *Lastly...*
   Secondly...   *Finally...*
   What's more...
   Another reason...   *For example...*
   Moreover...   *For instance...*
   In addition...   *e.g.,...*

Pair work   Student A should look at Activity 33 and Student B at 49.
Look carefully at this example first:

```
Importance of accuracy in English:
(1) exams (e.g., TOEFL), (2) writing (e.g., letters)
```

One reason why accuracy is important is that on many exams, for example
on the TOEFL, inaccuracy can lose points. Another reason is that when
you're writing something, for example a letter, mistakes can give a very bad
impression.

32 | *Word order*

32.1 Modifiers

A Look at these examples:

NUMBER	SIZE + QUALITY	COLOR OR PATTERN	NATIONALITY	MATERIAL	NOUN as modifier	NOUN
One	nice, new	red	Swiss	wool	ski	hat
Two	cheap, secondhand	white	American	cotton	sun	hats
Three	large, old	striped	Canadian	polyester	baseball	caps
Four	fantastic, modern	silver	Japanese	fiberglass	motorcycle	helmets

   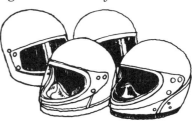

B Rearrange these words to make a correct phrase:

1. Five   winter   black   large   Italian   beautiful   **coats**
2. Six   brilliant   Mexican   film   young   **directors**
3. Seven   Korean   white   ceramic   valuable   flower   **vases**
4. Eight   pink   beautiful   cotton   Indonesian   tennis   **shirts**
5. Nine   house   lovely   Brazilian   green   bright   **plants**
6. Ten   plastic   wobbly   Swedish   strange   yellow   **bicycles**

32.2 Adverbs

A Look at the examples below, which show where different adverbs are most commonly placed in a sentence. Other, more emphatic, positions are sometimes possible.

BEFORE	MID-POSITION	AFTER
Suddenly I had a toothache.	I **suddenly** had a toothache.	
Soon I had a toothache.	I **soon** had a toothache.	
Yesterday I had a toothache.		I had a toothache **yesterday**.
Recently I had a toothache.	I **recently** had a toothache.	I had a toothache **recently**.
		I had a toothache **at the office**.
	I **certainly** had a toothache.	
	I **never** have toothaches.	

B   Put the adverbs and adverb phrases on the right into the sentences.
Some of them can be put into more than one place.

1. I'm going to France for my vacation.   probably
   I'm probably going to France for my vacation.
2. She was waiting for me.   indoors
3. He's leaving the country.   tomorrow
4. She sings and dances.   beautifully
5. They write to their parents.   once a week
6. I stayed in the library and worked.   hard
7. The door opened and a hand appeared.   slowly
8. He plays the piano.   very well
9. You'll have to run to catch the train.   fast
10. They hid the presents.   behind the sofa

32.3   Mid-position adverbs

A   The adverbs below usually go in mid-position. Look at the examples to
see what is meant by "mid-position."

*never   always   often   usually   rarely   hardly ever   frequently   ever
obviously   clearly   surely   probably   presumably   certainly   apparently
almost   nearly   completely   just   hardly   really*

*I **never** eat chocolates.*
*I don't **ever** eat chocolates.*
*I have **never** eaten chocolates.*
*These chocolates will **never** be eaten.*

B   Put the adverbs into the correct position in each sentence.

1. I've enjoyed Westerns.   *always*   6. We're going to be late.   *probably*
2. I've finished my work.   *just*   7. I can understand him.   *hardly*
3. You'll be met at the airport. *certainly*   8. She loses her temper.   *rarely*
4. He shouldn't have done that. *clearly*   9. It's quite difficult.   *obviously*
5. Oops! I fell over.   *nearly*   10. Things won't improve.   *ever*

32.4   Rearrange the words

Pair work   Rearrange the words in each line below to make a well-
known saying. Then decide when each saying might be used.

1. sword   The   mightier   pen   than   is   the
   The pen is mightier than the sword.
2. succeed, and   If   you   don't   again   at   first   try   try
3. Rome   day   built   in   wasn't   a
4. Rome   do   When   as   in   do   the   Romans
5. milk   no   use   It's   spilled   over   crying
6. cloud   silver   has   a   lining   Every
7. end   All   good   must   to   an   things   come

Grammar summaries

The following grammar summaries are for review and quick reference. They offer some useful "rules of thumb" and examples to help you to remember what you have practiced in each unit.

 If you need a more detailed explanation of the rules or further examples, consult a grammar reference book, such as *Grammar in Use* by Raymond Murphy (Cambridge University Press).

1 *Yes/No questions*

Question formation:

Are *you* **feeling** *all right?*
Is *this correct?*
Did *you* **go** *to the park in the afternoon?*
Can *I* **help** *you?*

Have *you ever* **eaten** *lobster?*
Were *you in class yesterday?*
Do *you* **play** *tennis?*

Negative questions (making sure that you are right):

Isn't *that your brother?*
Isn't *this correct?*
Can't *you* **swim?**

Didn't *she once* **live** *in Tokyo?*
Aren't *you* **feeling** *well?*
Haven't *you* **finished** *yet?*

2 *Wh- questions*

Different *Wh-* question words:

What. . . ?   Who. . . .?   Where. . . ?   When. . . ?   Which. . . ?   Why. . . ?   How. . . ?
How many. . . ?   How much. . . ?   What for. . . ?   What else. . . ?

Question formation:

How many cookies **have** *you* **eaten?**
Who **gave** *you the book?*
When **will** *you* **know?**

What **did** *you* **do** *yesterday?*
Who **did** *you* **give** *the book* **to?***
What time **does** *the flight* **leave?**

Indirect question formation – polite questions:

Could you tell me **where** *the museum* **is?**
I'd like to know **if** *you***'ve** *ever* **been** *to Korea.*
Would you mind telling me **what** *you* **did** *there?*

* Some people prefer these forms:
To whom *did you give the book?* or **Whom** *did you give the book* **to?**
but they are more common in writing and not often used in conversation.

3   *The past:* What happened?
The present perfect: What has happened?

Simple past:
  I **went** *to Brazil* **in 1990.**   *I* **enjoyed** *my visit to Rio* **in June.**
  I **didn't get up** *until 9 o'clock* **yesterday morning.**

Present perfect:
  Have *you* **ever been** *to Japan?*   *I've* **never been** *to Thailand.*
  Have *you* **written** *those letters* **yet?**   *I've* **already written** *the letters.*

Irregular verbs (see page 6):
  I'd like to **see** *the Amazon.*   *I* **saw** *the Nile last year.*
  I've never **seen** *the Mississippi.*

4   *The past continuous:* What was happening?
The present perfect continuous: What has been happening?

The past continuous describes activities that were happening at the same time:
  He **was watching** *TV while you* **were reading.**
  What **were** *you* **doing** *while I* **was waiting** *for you?*

The past continuous also describes actions that began before a point in time and continued after:
  What **were** *you* **doing** *at 9 o'clock this morning?*
  I **was driving** *to work at 8:45.*

The past continuous also describes interrupted actions:
  I **was cooking** *dinner when the telephone rang.*

The present perfect continuous describes events that started in the past and are still happening (especially with *since* and *for,* and after *How long . . .* questions):
  How long **have you been studying** *English?*
  I **have been living** *here* **for** *five years.*   (*five years* is a period of time)
  I've **been waiting** *here* **since** *six o'clock.*   (*six o'clock* is a point in time)

Different meanings of the simple past, past continuous, and past perfect:
  I **got** *out of bed when the alarm clock went off.*   (I got out of bed
     immediately after the alarm went off.)
  I **was getting** *out of bed when the alarm clock went off.*   (I started to get out
     of bed just before it went off.)
  I **had** *already* **gotten** *out of bed when the alarm clock went off.*   (I got out of bed.
     Then the alarm went off.)

5   *Past, present, and future*

Talking about recent, current, and future events:
*She **has had** lunch.*   (recent past)
*She **is having** lunch.*   (now)
*She **is going to have** lunch.*   (soon)

Talking about past activities and habits:
*There was a time when I **smoked** 50 cigarettes a day.*   (in the past)
*I **used to be** a heavy smoker.*   (but not anymore)
***Did** you **use to play** volleyball?*   (some time in the past)

Talking about current habits:
*I **don't smoke** anymore.*
*I only **watch** volleyball now.*

For and *since* + present perfect:
*I **haven't seen** him **since 1988**.*   (point in time)
*I **have been feeling** sick **for several days**.*   (period of time)

6   *Quantity*

Some nouns are "countable":
car(s)   fact(s)   dollar(s)   person(s)   people   woman/women   kid(s)
child/children   hour(s)   bottle(s)   slice(s)   etc.
*How **many** cars can you see?*
*That **is an** interesting fact.*

Other nouns are "uncountable":
traffic   information   work   time   beer   advice   bread   etc.
*How **much** traffic is there on the road?*
*This **is** interesting information.*   (but: *This is **an** interesting **piece of** information.*)
*My parents give me **too much** advice!*   (but: *They gave me a good **piece** of advice.*)

Notice that *money* and *news* are "uncountable," so we can say:
*So **much** of the news is depressing this week.*
*They don't spend as **much** money as we do.*
but not: *How many moneys do you have?*

Remember that *people, dollars,* and *cents* are countable:
***Only a few** people can afford a Porsche.*
***Not many** people own a Mercedes.*
*Premium gas costs **a few** cents **more** than unleaded.*

Some nouns can be either countable or uncountable, depending on their meaning:
*I'd like **a glass** of milk.*   *Windows are made of **glass**.*
*I'm going to buy **a paper**.* (= a newspaper)   *I need **some paper**.* (= to write on)

7 Articles – I

We use *a, an, some,* or *any* with countable nouns, when we don't have a particular thing or person in mind:
> *I'd like **a** banana or **an** orange, please.*
> *Would you like **some** bananas or **some** other fruit?*
> *Do you know how to drive **a** car?*
> *He has **a** sister, but he doesn't have **any** brothers.*

The refers to particular things or people we have in mind:
> **The** *banana I had was rotten, but* **the** *orange was good.*   *I've lost* **the** *keys to* **the** *car.*
> *At* **the** *end of* **the** *movie,* **the** *hero got married to* **the** *heroine.*

The is not usually used when referring to things or people in general:
> *I love bananas and oranges.*
> *Fruit is good for you, and oranges are best of all.*
> *I enjoy music and writing letters.*
> *Doctors get paid more than nurses.*

A or *an* is used before names of professions or occupations, but not before subjects studied:
> *She wants to be* **a** *doctor. That's why she's studying medicine.*

---

8 Articles – II

No article is used before names of continents, most countries, states, cities, lakes, islands, mountains, and streets:
> *Asia   Sweden   California   Chicago   Lake Ontario   Hokkaido*
> *Mount McKinley   Broadway   Hollywood Boulevard   Main Street   etc.*

Some exceptions are:
> *the USA / United States   the USSR / Soviet Union   the UK / United Kingdom*
> *the Netherlands   the Philippines   the Republic of China*
> *the People's Republic of China*

Many of the important places in a city or state that a tourist might visit (except museums and galleries) have no article:
> *Fisherman's Wharf   Central Park   Yosemite National Park*
> *Waikiki Beach   Alcatraz Island   etc.*

But we use *the* before groups of islands, groups of mountains, oceans and seas, rivers, hotels, and museums:
> **the** *Canary Islands*   **the** *Himalayas*   **the** *Pacific*   **the** *Caribbean*   **the** *Nile*
> **the** *Sheraton*   **the** *Smithsonian*   **the** *Maritime Museum*   etc.

The or *a* are left out in some prepositional phrases:
> *You should go to bed.*   *He's at work.*

but not in other prepositional phrases:
> *Stop looking out of* **the** *window.*   *I got this at* **a** *store near me.*

9 *Comparison*

The use of the comparative (*better, more interesting*, etc.):
*Brazil is much larger **than** Greece.*
*Canada is **less** humid **than** Brazil.*
*Greece isn't **as** cold **as** Canada.*
*Japan is **more** mountainous **than** Uruguay.*

The use of the superlative (*best, most interesting*, etc.):
*Jim is **the fattest** boy in the class.*
*Sue is **the most** intelligent person in the class.*
*Tom is **the least** intelligent person I know.*

So, such a, too, and *enough* are used in "result clauses":
*The box is **so** heavy **that** I can't lift it.*
*It's **such a** heavy box **that** I can't lift it.*
*It's **too** heavy for me to lift.*
*It's **not** light **enough** for me to lift.*

10 *Requests and obligation*

Making requests:
Would you mind *opening the door?*   **I'd like you to** *open the door.*
Could you *open the door, please?*   **Will you** *please open the door?*
Can you *please open the door?*

Asking for permission:
Would you mind if I *opened the door?*   **Do you mind if I** *open the door?*
May I *open the door, please?*   **Is it all right if I** *open the door?*
Can I *open the door?*   **Could I** *open the door, please?*

Talking about what is permitted and not permitted (forbidden):
*You **can't** smoke in here.*   *You **can** smoke outside.*
*You **aren't allowed to** smoke in here.*   *You **are allowed to** smoke outside.*
*You **aren't supposed to** smoke in here.*   **It's all right to** *smoke outside.*
*You**'d better not** smoke in here.*

Talking about obligation and lack of obligation:
*You **have to** fill out this form.*   *You **don't have to** write in capitals.*
*You**'ve got to** fill out this form.*   **There's no need to** *write in capitals.*
*You **should** fill out this form.*

11 *Ability*

Ability and inability:
>*You **can** swim, but I **can't**.*
>*I'**ll be able to** swim by the end of the summer.*
>*I **wish I could** swim as well as you can.*
>*It'**d be nice to be able to** swim.*

>*I**'m unable to** swim.*

>*I **was able to** jump across the stream.*
>*I **managed to** jump across the stream.*

>*I **wasn't able to** step over it.*
>*I **didn't manage to** step over it.*
>*I **couldn't** step over it.*

Getting help to do things:
>*I'**d need someone to help me** prepare a four-course meal for 12 guests.*
>*I'**d get someone to** do the dishes afterwards.*   *I'**d have** the menus printed for me.*

12 *Advice and suggestions*

Asking for advice:
>*Should I **invite** him to the party?*
>*Is it worth **inviting** him?*
>*I can't decide whether **to invite** him.*
>*Do you think I should **invite** him?*

>*Would it be a good idea **to invite** him?*
>*I'm wondering whether **to invite** him.*
>*Do you think I ought **to invite** him?*

Giving advice and making suggestions:
>*If I were you I'**d see** the doctor.*
>*My advice is **to see** the doctor.*
>*I'**d advise you to see** the doctor.*
>*Why don't you **see** the doctor?*

>*I think you ought **to see** the doctor.*
>*You'**d better see** the doctor.*
>*You could **see** the doctor.*
>*You should **see** the doctor.*

Advising someone *not* to do something:
>*If I were you **I wouldn't invite** her.*
>*It'**d be better not to invite** her.*
>*It isn't a good idea **to invite** her.*

>*I don't think you ought **to invite** her.*
>*You shouldn't **invite** her.*
>*I'**d advise you not to invite** her.*

13 *Doing* or *to do? – I*

-ing forms are often used as the subject of a sentence, or as part of a phrase
that acts as the subject:
>**Swimming** *is my favorite sport.*   **Being criticized** *is unpleasant.*

to . . . (the infinitive) is often used after adjectives:
>*It's fun **to swim** in the ocean.*   *It's unpleasant **to be** criticized.*

-ing forms are always used after a preposition:
>*She climbed up **without** hold**ing** on.*   *He opened it **by** hold**ing** it firmly.*

Some verbs are usually followed by *-ing*:
> *avoid   enjoy   detest   finish   keep*   etc.
> *I* **enjoy** *listen****ing*** *to music and read****ing*** *books.*

Some verbs are usually followed by *to . . .* :
> *choose   learn   manage   mean   need*   etc.
> *I've* **learned to** *type and* **to** *use a computer.*

Some verbs are usually followed by an object + *to . . .* :
> *allow   encourage   force   invite   teach*   etc.
> *He* **encouraged me to** *do it.*   *They* **forced her to** *answer the questions.*

Some verbs can be followed either by *-ing* or *to. . .* with no difference in meaning:
> *begin   start   like   continue*   etc.
> *It* **began** *rain****ing***.   *It* **began to** *rain.*

---

14   *Doing* or *to do?* – *II*

Some verbs are followed by the preposition *to* + *-ing*:
> *I'm* **looking forward to** *see****ing*** *you.*   *I've* **gotten used to** *be****ing*** *alone.*

Stop + *-ing* and *stop* + *to . . .* have different meanings:
> *He's stopped cough****ing*** *and sneez****ing****.*   (his cold is better now)
> *They stopped* **to** *look at the map.*   (they stopped in order to look at the map)

Remember and *forget* can be followed by *-ing* or by *to . . .* with different meanings:
> *I remember see****ing*** *her at the party.*   (it is still in my memory)
> *I remembered* **to** *lock the door.*   (I didn't forget to do it)

Let and *make* are followed by an object + the base form, while *allow* and *force* are followed by an object + *to . . .* :
> *Please* **let me see** *the photos.*   *We aren't* **allowed to park** *here.*
> *They* **made him confess.**   *They* **forced him to confess.**

---

15   *Prepositions* – *I*

Prepositions of place:
> *in   on   at   behind   in front of   beside   next to   between   among   below*
> *underneath   on top of   inside   outside   near   a long way from   across*
> *The missing wallet was* **underneath** *a pile of books* **behind** *my desk.*

Prepositional phrases that describe exact positions:
> *on / to the left of   on / to the right of   on the left-hand side of   on the side of*
> *on the edge of   on the other side of   in the corner of   at / on the corner of*
> *at the top of   at the bottom of   in the middle of   at the back of   at the front of*
> *It's* **in the corner of** *the room* **on the left-hand side of** *my desk.*
> *My house is* **on/at the corner of** *First and Maple Streets.*

Prepositions of motion and direction:

> They ran **through** the field and jumped **over** the fence.
> Are you going **past** the post office on your way **back from** the bank?

16 *Prepositions – II*

Describing routes:
>   *Turn left at…*   *Turn right at…*   *Go straight.*
>   *When you get to the…*   *When you've passed the…*

Some adjectives are usually followed by *about* or *of*:
>   *angry about, happy about, nervous about,* etc.
>   *afraid of, terrified of, scared of, proud of,* etc.

I'm worried **about** *the future.*   *I'm scared* **of** *flying.*

Some adjectives are usually followed by *at*:
>   *good at, brilliant at, terrible at, better at,* etc.

He's pretty good **at** *tennis and even better* **at** *volleyball.*

Some adjectives are followed by particular prepositions:
>   *interested in, polite to, different from, responsible for, sorry for,* etc.

I'm interested **in** *baseball.*   *I feel sorry* **for** *people with no home.*

17   *The future*

Different forms are used to talk about future events and activities:

You'll get cold if you don't wear a coat.	— PREDICTION
*I'm **going to** apply for a new job.*	— INTENTION
*She's **going to** have a baby.*	— CERTAINTY about a future event, based on situation now
*I'm **seeing** the dentist tomorrow.*	— ARRANGEMENT
*Their train **arrives** at 8:00.*	— TIMETABLE
I'll pay you tomorrow.	— PROMISE
*I **won't** forget our appointment.*	— PROMISE
I'll open the door for you.	— OFFER
***Will** you let me know soon, please?*	— REQUEST
***Shall** we stop here for lunch?*	— SUGGESTION

In a time clause or an *If* ... clause, *will* and *going to* are not used:

*I'll have lunch **when** they **arrive**.*   *We'll go out **if** it **doesn't rain**.*

18   *Possibility and probability*

Talking about probability and improbability:
It'll probably *rain.*   **It probably won't** *rain.*
It looks as if it'll *rain.*   **It doesn't look as if it'll** *rain.*
It's likely to *rain.*   **It's not likely to** *rain.*

Talking about certainty and impossibility:
I'm *absolutely* **sure it'll** *rain.*   **I'm** *absolutely* **sure it won't** *rain.*
It's sure to *rain.*   **It won't** *rain,* **that's for sure.**

Talking about possibility and uncertainty:
It may *rain.*   **There's a chance it'll** *rain.*

Judging the truth of statements:
It's probably *true.*   **It could be** *true.*
It sounds as if it's *true.*   **It can't be** *true.*
It must be *true.*

Judging the likelihood of past events:
It probably *happened.*   **It can't have** *happened.*
It might have *happened.*   **It could have** *happened.*

19 *Verbs + prepositions*

Some verbs are followed by different prepositions with different meanings:
   look for (try to find)   *look after* (take care of)   *look at* (observe)
   *I'm looking **for** my shopping list.   She looked **at** me as if I were crazy.*

Some verbs are followed by a particular preposition:
   *stare at   welcome someone to   introduce someone to someone else
   share something with someone   etc.*
   *He shared his Coke **with** her.   I couldn't help staring **at** them.*

Some verbs are followed by different prepositions before "someone" or "something":
   *argue with someone about something   speak to / with someone about something
   apologize to someone for doing something   etc.*
   *He **apologized** to her **for** breaking the glasses.*

20 *Phrasal verbs*

Phrasal verbs can be formed with a verb of motion + a "particle":
   VERBS: *jump, run, come, climb, drive, pull, push, bring, go, etc.*
   PARTICLES: *up, down, in, out, past, away, back, off, over, etc.*
   *The general saluted as the soldiers **marched past.***
   *Please **go away** and don't **come back.***
   *My dog **ran away** and we can't find him.*

Often it's not possible to work out the meaning of a phrasal verb from its parts:
   *I can't **make out** what they're saying.*   (I can't hear them/understand them clearly.)
   *My brother and I don't **get along**.*   (We aren't good friends.)
   *We **checked in** early for our flight.*   (We arrived early at the airport and showed our tickets.)

Some phrasal verbs are not followed by an object. Notice the word order here:
   *The plane **took off** on time.*   but not: *The plane took on time off.*
   *Roses **come out** in the summer.*   but not: *Roses come in the summer out.*
   *Let's **get together** next week.*   but not: *Let's get next week together.*

Some phrasal verbs are followed by an object. Notice the word order here:
   *Please **take** this soup **away**.*   *Please **take away** this soup.*
   *Please **take** it **away**.*   but not: *Please take away it.*
   *She **turned** the radio **on**.*   *She **turned on** the radio.*
   *She **turned** it **on**.*   but not: *She turned on it.*

Note: In some cases a verb + preposition (*take after, look like, stare at,* etc.)
may look like a phrasal verb. But notice the word order in these examples:
   *Ann **takes after** her father.*   but not: *Ann takes her father after.*
   *Ann **takes after** him.*   but not: *Ann takes him after.*
   *Tom **looks like** his mother.*   but not: *Tom looks his mother like.*
   *Tom **looks like** her.*   but not: *Tom looks her like.*

21 *If . . . sentences – I*

If . . . can be used in three different types of conditional sentences:

1. *If I* **see** *her, I'll* *tell her.*   (I may see her.)
   If I **see** *her, I* **won't** *forget to tell her.*   (I may see her.)
   If I **don't see** *her, I* **won't** *be able to tell her.*   (I may not see her.)

2. *If he* **were** *more friendly, he'd / he* **would** *be more popular.*   (He isn't friendly.)
   If they **were** *more friendly, we* **wouldn't** *dislike them.*   (They aren't friendly.)
   If she **weren't** *so friendly, she* **wouldn't** *be so popular.*   (She is friendly.)

3. *If I* **had known** *you won, I'd* **have**/*I* **would have** *congratulated you.*   (I didn't know.)
   If I **had known** *it was a secret, I* **wouldn't have** *told anyone.*   (I didn't know.)
   If we **hadn't** *turned on the TV, we* **wouldn't have** *seen the news.*   (We did turn it on.)

If . . . or *unless . . .* + present (as type 1 above):
   If I **wake up** *early, I'll* *go for a run.*
   If I **don't wake up** *early, I* **can't go** *for a run.*
   I **can't go** *for a run if I* **don't wake** *up early.*
   I **won't go** *for a run unless I* **wake** *up early.*

If . . . + past (as type 2 above)*:
   If he **knew** *more, he'd/he* **would pass** *the exam.*
   He'd/he **would pass** *the exam if he* **knew** *more.*
   If he **were** *more studious, he* **might pass** *the exam.*   (not: If he was more studious...)

If, unless, when, and *until* have different meanings:
   I'll make coffee **when** *they arrive.*   (They will arrive.)
   I'll make coffee **if** *they arrive.*   (But they may not come.)
   I won't make coffee **until** *they arrive.*   (Not before they come.)
   I won't make coffee **unless** *they arrive.*   (But they may not come at all.)

*Although this is the past form, it's the subjunctive tense.

22 *If . . . sentences – II*

Past conditionals (as in type 3 in Unit 21 above):
   If they **had known** *the truth, they* **might have** *been shocked.*   (They didn't know the truth.)
   If I **had known** *the price of the shoes, I* **wouldn't have** *tried them on.*   (I didn't know the price.)
   I **wouldn't have** *gone to the beach if I* **had heard** *the weather forecast.*   (I didn't hear it.)

In past conditionals, *had* and *would* can both be contracted to *'d*:
   If **I had** *known,* **I would have** *told you about it.*
   If **I'd** *known,* **I'd have** *told you about it.*

Sometimes "mixed" conditionals can be formed:
   If I **had been** *born 100 years ago, I* **wouldn't** *be here today.*
   If they **weren't** *so careless, they* **wouldn't have** *made those mistakes.*

23 & 24   *The passive – I & II*

Different forms of the passive:
"Hamlet" **was written** *by Shakespeare.*   (Shakespeare wrote "Hamlet.")
I think I'm **being followed.**   (I think someone is following me.)
Being laughed at *is unpleasant.*   (It's unpleasant if someone laughs at you.)
He **has been arrested.**   (The police have arrested him.)

The passive is sometimes used to describe actions where the person
responsible is unknown or unimportant:
She **has been promoted.**   (by her boss, presumably)
He **was given** *a raise last month.*   (by his company)

25   *Prepositional phrases – I*

Preposition + noun expressions:
in bed   in pencil   by heart   by accident
on vacation   on purpose   at home   at school
out of date   out of sight
I lay **in** *bed* **at** *home trying to learn the words* **by** *heart.*

Prepositional phrases can be used to describe various ways of traveling:
for a drive   for a walk   on a trip   on a tour
by car   by train   on a train   on a bus
on the train   on the bus   in a train   in a bus
in the train   in the bus
Normally I come **by** *bus /* **on the** *bus, but today I came* **on** *foot.*

26   *Prepositional phrases – II*

Prepositional phrases with *time:*
on time   in time   at the same time   behind the times   etc.
He never arrives **on** *time.   He arrived* **in** *time for the meal.*

Preposition + noun + preposition expressions:
in addition to   in time for   in charge of   etc.
Sue's **in charge of** *the office while the boss is away.*

Some prepositional phrases can be used to connect sentences:
on the one hand ... on the other hand   for example   in theory   etc.
I don't know what to think of this book. **On the one hand** *it's very well
written, but* **on the other hand** *it's way too long.*

27 *Reported speech: statements*

Statements made recently are normally reported with verbs in the present tense:
> *"I'm feeling sick."* → *She **says that** she's feeling sick.*
> *"It's too difficult."* → *She **thinks that** it's too difficult.*

Statements made some time ago are reported with verbs in the past tense:
> *"It'll be difficult."* → *He **said that** it **would** be difficult.*
> *"It's a long way."* → *He **told me that** it **was** a long way.*

That can be omitted when reporting statements:
> *She **says** she's feeling sick.* *He **said** it **would** be difficult.*

28 *Reported speech: questions and requests*

Questions are reported with a change in word order from direct speech:
> *"Is it true?"* → *He asked me **if it was** true.*
> *"When is it going to happen?"* → *He wanted to know **when it was** going to happen.*

Requests, orders, advice, and invitations are reported using *to . . . :*
> *"Please open the door."* → *She asked me **to** open the door.*
> *"You should stop smoking."* → *She advised me **to** stop smoking.*
> *"Would you like to come?"* → *She invited me **to** come.*

29 *Relative clauses*

"Identifying" relative clauses contain essential information. "Nonidentifying" relative clauses contain extra, nonessential information, sometimes added as an afterthought. Notice the use of **commas** with "nonidentifying" relative clauses.

"Identifying" relative clauses are formed using *who, that, which, where,* or *whose*:
> *He is the man **who** I told you about.** *He is the man **that** I told you about.*
> *This is the book **that** you need.* *This the book **which** you need.*
> *She's the girl **whose** mother won the prize.*
> *He has two sons: The son **who** is a doctor lives in San Francisco.*

Who, that, and *which* can be left out if they are the objects of an "identifying" relative clause:
> *He is the man I told you about.* *This is the book you need.*

"Nonidentifying" relative clauses are formed using *who, which, where, when,* or *whose*:
> *Her mother, **who** is 67, likes candy.* *My house, **which** is very old, is falling to pieces.*
> *The year 1812, **when** Napoleon went to Russia, was very significant.*

* Some people prefer to use *whom* here, but this is more common in writing and not often used in conversation:
> *He is the man **whom** I told you about.* or *He is the man about **whom** I told you.*

Who and *which* can be used to connect sentences:
> *She is very shy,* **which** *I find surprising.*
> *I'm in love with Chris,* **who** *is a wonderful person.*

---

30 *Joining sentences – I*

Different verb forms used with *when* in time clauses:
> *I* **spoke** *to him when he* **arrived**.
> *I'll* **speak** *to him when he* **arrives**.
> *I* **started** *my dinner when he* **left/had left**. (He left, then I started eating.)
> *I* **had started** *dinner when he* **left**. (I started, then he left.)

Different time conjunctions can be used in time clauses:
> *as, until, by the time, whenever, while, as soon as, since,* etc.
> *She phoned me* **as** *I was having breakfast.*
> *I always feel sick* **before** *an exam.*

Conjunctions can be used to join sentences in different ways:
> *I've brought my umbrella* **in case** *it rains.*   (precaution)
> *I've brought my umbrella* **because** *it's raining.*   (reason)
> *You don't need an umbrella* **unless** *it's raining.*   (condition)
> *I've brought an umbrella* **so that** *I don't get wet.*   (purpose)
> *I've brought an umbrella* **even though** *it's not raining.*   (contrast)

---

31 *Joining sentences – II*

Related nouns or pronouns can be connected with coordinating structures:
> **Both** *Bill* **and** *his sister came.*   *Bring* **either** *soda* **or** *juice.*
> **Neither** *Mary* **nor** *John came.*   **None of** *the family came* **except** *Jane.*

Adverbs of time can be used to link two separate sentences together:
> *She had a great time at the party.* **Meanwhile** *I was at home studying.*
> *He left at 6:30.* **Before that** *we'd taken a long walk.*
> *We had a wonderful meal.* **Afterwards** *we had to do the dishes.*

Other adverb phrases can be used to link two separate sentences together:
> *I hate bananas.* **That's why** *I never eat fruit salad.*   (reason)
> *I love oranges.* **Nevertheless,** *I hate having to peel them.*   (contrast)
> *You could have ice cream for dessert.* **On the other hand,** *you could have fruit.*   (alternative)

Some adverb phrases can be used to connect several sentences together in
a paragraph:
> **In the first place,** *I don't like cooking very much.* **In fact,** *I hate it.* **What's**
> **more,** *I find that spending hours in the kitchen is exhausting.*

32 *Word order*

Adjectives and other words that come before a noun are usually arranged in this order:

1	2	3	4	5	6	7
NUMBER	SIZE + QUALITY	COLOR OR PATTERN	NATIONALITY	MATERIAL	NOUN as modifier	NOUN
two	*beautiful*	*brown*	*Greek*	*ceramic*	*water*	*pitchers*

Some adverbs are normally placed in "mid-position" in a sentence:

    I have **never** *eaten oysters.*   *I can* **never** *eat oysters.*
    I **never** *eat oysters.*   *I'll* **never** *eat oysters.*

(Other "mid-position" adverbs are: *always, often, almost, hardly, rarely,* etc. – see page 65.)

Other adverbs fit more comfortably at the beginning or end of a sentence:

    Yesterday *I went to the zoo.*   *I went to the zoo* **yesterday**.
    Recently *I traveled to Rome.*   *I traveled to Rome* **recently**.

but some of these adverbs also fit in mid-position:

    I **recently** *traveled to Rome.*

Note: It is best to rely on your own feelings for what sounds right or "comfortable," rather than try to memorize complex rules of word order.

Communication activities

Answer your partners' questions about this photograph:

1

Some information is missing from the lists below. Ask your partner questions to find out the missing information.

2

For example: *Who was born in .... ?*   *When did .... die?*
                Who died in .... ?   *When was .... born?*

You can also ask questions like these:
   What did .... do in his / her life?   *What did .... become famous for?*
   What is .... remembered for today?

Births		*Deaths*	
1770	Beethoven	18	Beethoven
1819	....	1901	Queen Victoria
1820	Susan B. Anthony	1906	....
1867	Marie Curie	....	Mata Hari
1876	Mata Hari	1934	....
1879	Albert Einstein	1937	Amelia Earhart
1884	Eleanor Roosevelt	1955	James Dean + ...
1889	Charlie Chaplin	1962	Marilyn Monroe + ...
1897	Amelia Earhart	1977	Elvis Presley + ...
1926	....		
....	James Dean		
1935	....		

3   Find out if your partner has ever done any of the things shown below.
If the answer is *Yes*, then find out *When ...?*
and *What was it like?*
and *What happened?*

Ever		Ever	
	ridden a motorcycle?		driven a delivery van?
	been to Disneyland?		been skiing?
	been caught in a hurricane?		tried surfing?
	eaten lobster?		read a novel in English?
	given a speech?		taken a cruise?
	visited a Latin American country?		won a race or contest?
	climbed a mountain?		baked a cake?
	voted in an election?		stayed up all night?

When you answer your partner's questions, it might be more fun to invent a story
than to talk about what you really did.

4   Ask for your partner's views on these topics:

art galleries	Japanese food
Italian food	folk music
taking vitamins	traveling by subway
staying in shape	learning foreign languages
reading novels	taking a vacation in Europe
going to Disneyland	walking in the mountains

5   Answer your partners' questions about this photograph:

Find out if your partners think these statements are true by asking: **6**
"Do you think it's true that . . . ?"

1. Cats can't taste sweet things.
2. More babies are born on Sunday in the United States than on any other day of
   the week.
3. Horses don't breathe through their mouths.
4. Mirrors absorb 20% of light on each reflection.
5. Crocodiles don't chew their food, but swallow it whole. They grind it up with
   small stones they keep in their stomachs.
6. People can only distinguish three tastes.
7. Alaska is bigger than Texas, California, Florida, and New York combined.

(Your teacher has the correct answers.)

Imagine that you took your car to be serviced at your local garage, and these are **7**
the jobs you wanted them to do. Phone the garage and find out from your partner
which jobs have been done.

check oil
polish hood
install new rear tires
wash windshield
adjust carburetor

fix door lock
replace broken headlight bulb
change spark plugs
clean out trunk
fill tank with gas

When you have finished, turn to Activity 27 for the second part of this
communication activity.

Imagine that you and your partner are on a camping trip. Find out what supplies **8**
your partner still has left. Then say what you have left. Follow this pattern:

A: *Do you have any* ....*rice*......... *left?*
B: *Yes. How much would you like?*   OR   *How many* ....*packets*..... *would you like?*
A: ..*Four packets*.. *please.*   OR   .....*Four*..... *please.*
B: *I'm sorry, I only have* ....*two*.......... OR   *Here you are!*

Things you have run out of:	*Things you still have left:*
rice	lemonade (12)
chocolate	sugar (2)
bread	matches (4)
soap	toothpaste (4)
gum	milk (½)
honey	salt (1)

9   Find out if your partner has ever done any of the things shown below. If the answer is *Yes*, then find out *When ...?*

and *What was it like?*
and *What happened?*

Ever driven a sports car?	Ever drunk goat's milk?
been abroad?	cooked a meal for a family?
been caught in a thunderstorm?	visited a European country?
eaten snails?	eaten raw fish?
failed an exam?	been water skiing?
tried windsurfing?	been given a fabulous present?
acted in a play?	gotten hopelessly lost?
saved someone's life?	found some money in the street?

When you answer your partner's questions, it might be more fun to invent a story than to talk about what you really did.

10   *Part 1*   You're going to do several things that may annoy your partner. Do each thing shown here until your partner asks you to stop.

whistle   whisper to yourself   sigh   sniff   clear your throat

Then your partner is going to annoy you. Ask your partner to stop by saying:
   "Please stop whistling."   or   *"Would you mind not whistling?"*

Part 2   Tell your partner about a long walk that you once went on. You had to make several stops along the way, and you'll have to explain these:

1st stop: drink   2nd stop: looked at map   3rd stop: made a phone call
4th stop: meal   5th stop: met a friend   6th stop: bought some ice cream

Your conversation should go like this:

Your partner: *Why did you make your first stop?*
YOU: *I stopped to get a drink. I was very thirsty.*
Your partner: *Oh. And then what did you do?*
YOU: *After getting a drink I went on walking, but soon I stopped again.*
Your partner: *Why did you stop again?*

Then find out about the walk that your partner went on.

11   Ask for your partner's views on these topics:

watching television	pollution	reading magazines
Mexican food	traveling by bus	playing golf
having a credit card	Chinese food	skiing
jazz	classical music	taking a cruise

Answer your partners' questions about this photograph:

12

First give the following instructions to your partner. Try to use the expressions on page 20.

13

> Raise both of your hands to shoulder level. Put them both out in front of you. Now put them behind your neck. Stand up. Put your left hand on your right shoulder. Put your right hand on your left hip. Wink with your left eye. Then with your other eye. Sit down again. Close your eyes. Open them very wide. Now relax. Thank you.

Begin like this: *"First of all, I'd like you to raise both of your hands ..."*

When you have finished, follow your partner's instructions.

Kumiko wears glasses.
Beth plays tennis.
Carol has long blonde hair.
Maria has a baby.

Linda was in your class at school.
Erica used to sing in a rock group.
Sue used to be a fashion model.
Jane was your sister's best friend at school.

14

15

Some information is missing from the lists below. Ask your partner questions to find out the missing information.

For example: *Who was born in .... ?* *When did .... die?*
Who died in .... ? *When was .... born?*

You can also ask questions like these:
What did .... do in his/her life? *What did .... become famous for?*
What is .... remembered for today?

Births		Deaths	
17 ...		1827	Beethoven
1819	Queen Victoria	1901	....
1820	....	1906	Susan B. Anthony
1867	....	1917	Mata Hari
....	Mata Hari	1934	Marie Curie
1879	....	1937	....
....	Eleanor Roosevelt	1955	Albert Einstein + ...
1889	....	1962	Eleanor Roosevelt + ...
1897	....	1977	Charlie Chaplin + ...
1926	Marilyn Monroe		
1931	James Dean		
1935	Elvis Presley		

16

Part 1 Find out if your partner did these things that he or she promised to do:
do the shopping *phone the hairdresser* *pay the rent*
pick up the drycleaning *write a composition*

These are some things you were supposed to do, which you either remembered to do (✔) or forgot to do (✗).
mail the letter ✗ *buy a newspaper* ✔ *go to the bank* ✗
get some gas ✔ *buy some stamps* ✗

Use some of these phrases in your conversation:
Did you remember to ... ? *I'm afraid I forgot to ...* *I did remember to ...*
I bet you forgot to ... *I didn't remember to ...* *I didn't forget to ...*

Part 2 Share these memories with your partner. Ask about your partner's memories of the same occasions:
a holiday celebration in your country your first date
going abroad for the first time a wedding you went to
your first English lesson the first movie you ever saw

Use some of these phrases in your conversation:
I'll always remember ... *Do you remember ...?*
I'll never forget ... *What do you remember about ...?*

Part 1   Your partner is going to do some things that annoy you. Ask your partner to stop by saying:

17

   "Please stop tapping."   or   *"Would you mind not staring?"*

Now you're going to do several things that may annoy your partner. Continue doing each thing shown here until your partner asks you to stop.

   tap your foot   *stare at your partner*   *doodle*   *hum a tune*   *click your tongue*

Part 2   Your partner will tell you about a long walk that she or he once went on. Ask questions about it.

Then tell your partner about a walk that YOU took. You had to make several stops along the way, and you'll have to explain these:

   1st stop: asked directions   2nd stop: rest   3rd stop: admired the view
   4th stop: got out of the rain   5th stop: picnic
   6th stop: bought bandage for sore toe

Your conversation should go like this:

Your partner: *Why did you make your first stop?*
YOU: *I stopped to ask for directions. I was lost.*
Your partner: *Oh. And then what did you do?*
YOU: *After asking for directions I went on walking, but soon I stopped again.*
Your partner: *Why did you stop again?*

Don't tell your partner what this picture shows! Tell your partner to use the grid of numbers on page 31. Then explain the "route" your partner's pencil should take to draw the picture below.

18

Begin like this: *"Start at number 1 and draw a line through number 12. Stop the line just above number 23. Now draw the line above numbers 23 through 28 … "*

Start here

1	2	3	4	5	6	7	8	9	10
11	12	13	14	15	16	17	18	19	20
21	22	23	24	25	26	27	28	29	30
31	32	33	34	35	36	37		39	40
41	42	43	44	45	46	47	48	49	50
51	52	53	54	55	56	57	58	59	60
61	62	63	64	65	66	67	68	69	70
71	72	73	74	75	76	77	78	79	80
81	82	83	84	85	86	87	88	89	90
91	92	93	94	95	96	97	98	99	100

19

These are the instructions that were left for the painters.
You can see what was done right: blue ✓
and what was done wrong: white — *pale green* (= pale green instead of white)

	DOOR	WALLS	CEILING
Kitchen	blue ✓	~~white~~ — pale green	~~white~~ — pink
Study	dark green ✓	~~pale green~~ — white	~~green~~ — red
Living room	tan ✓	~~tan~~ — brown	~~white~~ — tan
Hall	~~blue~~ — red	pale blue ✓	~~gray~~ — blue
Front door	~~white~~ — gray		
Bedroom	~~orange~~ — red	orange ✓	white ✓
Bathroom	~~white~~ — blue	~~blue~~ — white	pale blue ✓

> Was your kitchen painted all right?

> No, the kitchen ceiling should have been painted white instead of pink. And the walls were painted pale green instead of white.

> And how about the door?

> The door was painted blue, which was fine.

20

Find out from your partner about what everyone is doing in his or her picture. Ask what the people did earlier and what they are going to do next.

Then tell your partner about the picture below. Explain to your partner what the people did earlier and what they are going to do next.

First follow the instructions your partner gives you. Then give the following instructions to your partner. Try to use the expressions on page 20.

21

Raise your right hand. Place it on your left knee. Lift your left leg three inches from the floor. Stand up. Remove your right hand from your knee. Press both feet closely together. Wave your left hand loosely by your side. Do the same with your other hand. Keep both arms waving loosely and sit down. Now keep completely still for 15 seconds without blinking. Relax. Thank you.

Begin like this: *"First of all, I'd like you to raise your right hand ..."*

Don Quixote has a dream of being a perfect knight.
In *Batman*, a wealthy man dresses as a bat and fights crime.
E.T. is a creature from outer space.
The family in *100 Years of Solitude* experiences magical happenings in their South American town.
In *Tampopo* a widow tries to run a noodle shop outside Tokyo.

22

Imagine that you have been shopping for the items on List 1 (on page 22). Unfortunately, you haven't been able to buy the exact items on the list. Tell your partner about this.

23

a dozen large eggs — *only small available — got those*
1 bag of carrots ✓ — *very nice ones!*
1 jar of grape jelly — *No, got strawberry jam instead*
2 small loaves of whole wheat bread — *No, got 1 large one*
2 pounds of cheese — *No fresh cheese in the store today*
1 jar of instant coffee ✓ — *Special offer: got 2 for the price of one!*
3 large cans of soup — *None in the store — not even small ones*

Now look at List 2 on page 22. Find out if your partner managed to get everything on the list.

24

Find out if your partners think these statements are true by asking: "Do you think it's true that . . . ?"

1. Children born in May are 200 grams heavier at birth than children born in any other month.
2. Your nose and ears don't stop growing till you are 40.
3. It takes 17 muscles to smile and 43 to frown.
4. On a clear moonlit night, a person on a mountain peak can see a match struck 50 miles away.
5. Two out of three adults in the United States wear glasses at some time.
6. If you get wet and very cold, you are more likely to catch a cold.
7. California has more people than any other state in the United States.

(Your teacher has the correct answers.)

25

Linda has curly hair.
Sue rides a motorcycle.
Erica plays the violin.
Jane is a flight attendant.

Kumiko and you met in Tokyo two years ago.
Carol used to go out with your brother.
Maria used to work with your sister.
Beth went to the same school as you.

26

Part 1   These are some things you were supposed to do, which you either remembered to do (✓) or forgot to do (✗).
do the shopping ✓   *phone the hairdresser* ✗   *pay the rent* ✓
pick up the drycleaning ✗   *write a composition* ✗

Find out if your partner did these things that she or he promised to do:
mail the letter   *buy a newspaper*   *go to the bank*   *get some gas*
buy some stamps

Use some of these phrases in your conversation:
Did you remember to ... ?   *I'm afraid I forgot to ...*   *I did remember to ...*
I bet you forgot to ...   *I didn't remember to ...*   *I didn't forget to ...*

Part 2   Share these memories with your partner. Ask about your partner's memories of the same occasions:
trying a favorite food for the first time   a vacation you enjoyed
the first time you flew in an airplane   using a computer for the first time
your first conversation with an   meeting your partner for the first
   English-speaking person   time

Use some of these phrases in your conversation:
I'll never forget ...   *What do you remember about ...?*
I'll always remember ...   *Do you remember ...?*

Imagine that you stayed home today to get things ready for a dinner party. Your partner is going to call you to check which jobs have been done. The things that have been done are shown with a check (✓).

27

prepare vegetables ✓   *weigh ingredients* ✓
make sauce   *wash rice*
buy fruit ✓   *open wine* ✓
polish glasses   *set table*
find napkins ✓   *clean dining room*

Imagine that you have been shopping for the items on List 2 (on page 22). Unfortunately, you haven't been able to buy the exact items on the list. Tell your partner about this.

28

1 large roll of Scotch tape — had to get two small rolls
1 box of paper clips ✔
2 cassettes (C90) — got 2 C60s instead
2 red ballpoint pens — No, but got 1 blue one
4 size AA batteries — could only get 2
1 pack of airmail envelopes — No, only ordinary ones, so didn't get any
1 large box of staples ✔ — but lost it!!

Now look at List 1 on page 22. Find out if your partner got everything on the list.

Rewrite this reported conversation in dialogue form. Show only the names of the speakers (Dan and Kathy), and give the exact words they said. This is Dan's version:

29

I mentioned to Kathy that I was dating Lucy. Kathy immediately told me to phone Lucy and break up with her. I was pretty shocked, to say the least. I said she had no right to interfere with my personal life. She just laughed and told me not to be silly. Well, of course, I told her to get out and leave me alone. At first she refused, but finally I persuaded her to go.

Dan: You know, I'm dating Lucy.
Kathy: What? Call her right now and ...

30

Find out if your partners think these statements are true by asking: "Do you think it's true that . . . ?"

1. Babies can breathe and swallow at the same time but adults can't.
2. The feet of a housefly are 10 times more sensitive to sugar than a person's tongue.
3. It is impossible to sneeze and keep your eyes open at the same time.
4. In New York City the rats outnumber the people by 2 to 1.
5. Cuddling cats and dogs makes us feel good, but it can also give us more than 30 diseases.
6. People who smoke cigarettes have 10% more motor vehicle accidents than nonsmokers.
7. Alaska has fewer people than any other state in the United States.

(Your teacher has the correct answers.)

31

Tell your partner what everyone is doing in this picture. Describe what the people did earlier, and what they are going to do next.

Then find out about your partner's picture. Ask what happened earlier and what's going to happen next.

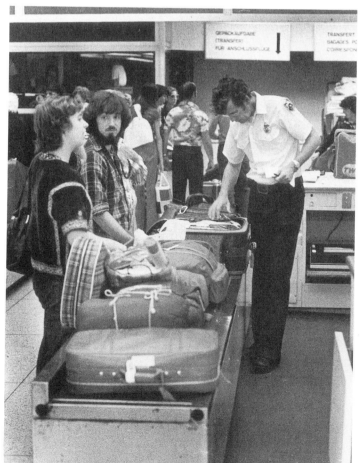

Imagine that you ran into your old school friend Mary the other day. She told you all about John, her husband. This is what she said to you:

32

> John and I have been married for eight years.
> I first got to know him at a friend's birthday party.
> But we had been introduced some time before that.
> He arrived at the party very late.
> He didn't recognize me when he asked me to dance.
> I told him that I didn't really want to dance.
> Although he was a terrible dancer, we danced all night.
> We didn't leave the party till dawn.
> We went out together every evening that week.
> We got married about six months later – on July 7th.
> I'll never forget our honeymoon: It rained all the time.
> And we've managed to stay together ever since
>   – in spite of having fights almost every week!

Report this conversation to your partner, who has been talking to John. Compare what you both heard.

Tell your partner the advantages and disadvantages of the following activities. When you talk about advantages, your partner will mention some disadvantages, and vice versa.

33

REASONS FOR NOT GOING ABROAD ON A BUS TOUR:
1. don't see the *real* country
2. stuck with strangers
3. can't go anywhere by yourself

REASONS FOR GOING TO LIVE ABROAD:
1. can see the *real* country
2. experience new culture firsthand
3. can learn the language

REASONS FOR NOT BUYING A TELEVISION:
1. most programs are terrible (e.g., soap operas, game shows)
2. better news coverage in the newspapers
3. no time for other hobbies

REASONS FOR OWNING A CAR:
1. independence (e.g., go where and when you like)
2. enjoyment of driving
3. friends who need rides

REASONS FOR HAVING A CREDIT CARD:
1. don't have to carry lots of cash (e.g., when traveling)
2. can reserve hotel rooms, buy airline tickets, etc., by phone
3. can use all over the world

34

Imagine that you work at a garage. Your partner is going to phone you to check which jobs have been done to his or her car. The jobs that have been done are shown with a check (✓).

check oil ✓
polish hood
install new rear tires
wash windshield ✓
adjust carburetor ✓

fix door lock ✓
replace broken headlight bulb ✓
change spark plugs
clean out trunk ✓
fill tank with gas

When you have finished, turn to Activity 43 for the second part of this activity.

35

Imagine that you and your partner are old friends. As far as you remember, five years ago…

YOUR PARTNER used to:		and YOU used to:	
play the piano	drink a lot of milk	play the guitar ✓	drink mineral water ✓
go jogging	go to the theater	go for long walks	go to the movies ✓
be a lifeguard	play tennis	be a waiter/waitress	play basketball ✓
go out with Pat	ride a racing bike	go out with Chris	ride a motorcycle
have longer hair	listen to jazz	have shorter hair	listen to rock music ✓
go water skiing	swim every day	have a sailboat ✓	work out every day
		— The things you *still do* are checked (✓) above	

36

Prince Hamlet wants to kill his father's murderer.
In *Kramer versus Kramer* a divorced husband tries to raise his son by himself.
King Kong, an enormous ape, is captured on a remote island and brought to New York.
The family in *Dallas* lives in Texas and runs an oil business.
In *Frankenstein* a scientist creates a creature that resembles a human.

Rewrite this reported conversation in dialogue form. Show only the names of the speakers (Dan and Kathy), and give the exact words they said. This is Kathy's version:

37

> *I tried to find out what Dan was planning to do about Lucy, but he kept on saying he didn't know. Well, I told him to make up his mind. He asked me for my advice, so I told him to phone her and call the whole thing off. He seemed very upset. I said I had to go because I had things to do, but he wanted me to stay and comfort him. So I said goodbye and left, even though he was still trying to persuade me to stay.*

Kathy: What are you planning to do about Lucy, Dan?
Dan: I don't know. I have no idea.

Ask your partner to react to each of the following promises, threats, and offers.

38

If you like, I'll ...
   send you a postcard.
   tell you a story.
   bake you a cake.
   drive you to the airport.
   wake you up at 5 a.m.

If we're not careful, someone will ...
   punish us.
   shout at us.
   give us extra work to do.
   tell us off.

Then react to what your partner says to you, using the expressions on page 49.

Imagine that you and your partner are on a camping trip. Find out what supplies your partner still has left. Then say what you have left. Follow this pattern:

39

B: *Do you have any ....salt........ left?*
A: *Yes. How much would you like?* OR *How many ....packets...... would you like?*
B: *..Two packets.... please.* OR *....Two.... please.*
A: *I'm sorry, I only have ....one...... OR Here you are!*

Things you have run out of:

salt
lemonade
matches
milk
sugar
toothpaste

Things you still have left:

chocolate (4)
gum (2 packs)
bread (6 slices)
honey (2)
soap (2)
rice (2)

40

Imagine that you ran into your old school friend John the other day. He told you all about Mary, his wife. This is what he said to you:

> *I've known Mary for six years now.*
> *We first met at a New Year's Eve party.*
> *We both arrrived at the party at the same time.*
> *I asked her to dance, but we only had one dance.*
> *She told me that I was great dancer but that she felt tired.*
> *So we sat down and started talking.*
> *We made a date to meet again the next week.*
> *Then we left the party separately.*
> *We seemed to get along very well when we met again.*
> *We got married on July 17th.*
> *We went to the Canary Islands for our honeymoon: The weather was great.*
> *So we've been happily married ever since.*
> *And we haven't had a single fight in all those years – we're the perfect couple!*

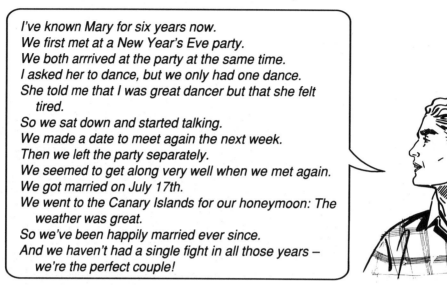

Report this conversation to your partner, who has been talking to Mary. Compare what you both heard.

41

Describe these three uncles to your partner. Use these structures:

Both Uncle Jack and Uncle Leo . . .
Neither Uncle Jack nor Uncle Leo . .
Uncle Dave doesn't have either
  a . . . or a . . .

UNCLE DAVE   UNCLE JACK   UNCLE LEO

42

First react to what your partner says to you, using the expressions on page 49.

Then ask your partner to react to each of the following promises, threats, and offers.

If we're not careful, someone will ...	*If you like, I'll ...*
criticize us.	*give you a present.*
swear at us.	*sing to you.*
blame us.	*treat you to lunch.*
laugh at us.	*tell you a joke.*
scream at us.	*show you my color slides.*

Imagine that your partner stayed home today to get things ready for a party.
Call your partner and find out which of the jobs in this list have been done.

43

prepare vegetables   weigh ingredients
make sauce   wash rice
buy fruit   open wine
polish glasses   set table
find napkins   clean dining room

In the musical *Cats* all the actors dress and act like cats.
Superman can fly and has other superhuman powers.
In *Gone with the Wind* a rich family is caught up in the American Civil War.
The detective Sherlock Holmes solved many mysteries based on very little evidence.
Romeo and Juliet can't marry because their families hate each other.

44

Don't tell your partner what this picture shows! Tell your partner to use the
grid of numbers on page 31. Then explain the "route" your partner's pencil
should take to draw the picture below.

45

Begin like this: *"Start at number 100. Draw a line through 100 and draw
upward to the left of 90, 80, and 70 ... "*

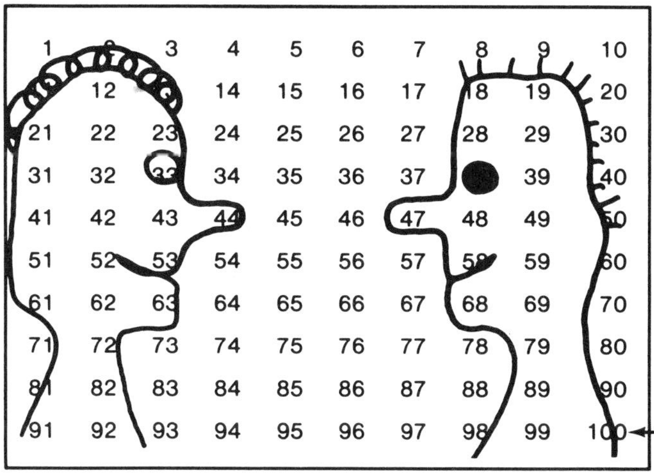

Start here

46

Describe these three uncles to your partner. Use these structures:

Both Uncle Steve and Uncle Ron . . .
Neither Uncle Steve nor Uncle Ron . . .
Uncle Bob doesn't have either a . . . or a . . .

47

These are the instructions that were left for the painters.
You can see what was done right: green ✓
and what was done wrong: yellow − white (= white instead of yellow)

	DOOR	WALLS	CEILING
Kitchen	green ✓	~~yellow~~ − white	~~pink~~ − red
Bathroom	~~blue~~ − white	~~white~~ − blue	pale blue ✓
Bedroom	~~yellow~~ − white	~~orange~~ − red	tan ✓
Front door	~~gray~~ − white		
Hall	blue ✓	~~pale blue~~ − red	white ✓
Living room	~~white~~ − blue	white ✓	~~white~~ − gray
Study	~~pale green~~ − red	dark green ✓	~~green~~ − red

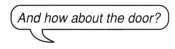

Was your kitchen painted all right?

No, the kitchen ceiling should have been painted red instead of pink. And the walls were painted yellow instead of white.

And how about the door?

The door was painted green, which was fine.

Imagine that you and your partner are old friends. As far as you remember, five years ago…

48

YOUR PARTNER used to:		and YOU used to:	
play the guitar	drink mineral water	play the piano ✓	drink a lot of milk
go for long walks	go to the movies	go jogging	go to the theater ✓
be a waiter/waitress	play basketball	be a lifeguard	play tennis ✓
go out with Chris	ride a motorcycle	go out with Pat	ride a racing bike
have shorter hair	listen to rock music	have longer hair	listen to jazz ✓
have a sailboat	work out every day	go water skiing ✓	swim every day ✓

— The things you *still do* are checked (✓) above

Tell your partner the advantages and disadvantages of the following activities. When you talk about advantages, your partner will mention some disadvantages, and vice versa.

49

REASONS FOR GOING ABROAD ON A BUS TOUR:
1. cheaper than traveling alone
2. easy to make friends
3. knowledgeable person serves as your guide

REASONS FOR NOT GOING TO LIVE ABROAD:
1. may miss your own country
2. may be lonely
3. difficult to make new friends

REASONS FOR BUYING A TELEVISION:
1. many good programs (e.g., documentaries, movies)
2. can be educational
3. good, inexpensive entertainment

REASONS FOR NOT OWNING A CAR:
1. quicker to travel on public transportation (e.g., bus, train, subway)
2. expensive to maintain
3. you can get rides from friends who own cars

REASONS FOR NOT HAVING A CREDIT CARD:
1. problems if it gets stolen
2. encourages people to spend more than they have
3. expensive to have one (e.g., annual fee, finance charges)

Acknowledgments

Illustrators

Chris Evans   pages 17 (*top*), 64 (*top*), 73

Noel Ford   pages 39 (*top*), 45 (*bottom*), 51 (*bottom*), 61 (*bottom*), 65 (*bottom*)

Mark Kaufman   pages 31, 46

David McKee   page 44 (*bottom*)

Robert Melendez   pages 4 (*bottom*), 13, 14, 15 (*bottom*), 20 (*bottom*), 21, 27, 28 (*top*), 29, 39 (*bottom*), 40 (*bottom*), 44 (*top*), 45 (*top*), 47 (*top*), 48, 49 (*top*), 51 (*top*), 61 (*top*), 93, 96 (*top*)

Wally Neibart   pages 6, 12, 15 (*top*), 17 (*bottom*), 18 (*top: heads*), 19 (*bottom*), 20 (*top*), 23, 26, 30 (*top*), 37 (*bottom*), 40 (*top*), 41, 49 (*bottom*), 50, 55 (*top*), 57, 59, 62, 63, 64 (*bottom*), 65 (*top, middle*), 96 (*bottom*), 98

Dave Parkins   page 18 (*top: animals*)

Bill Thomson   pages 2, 3, 9 (*top*), 11, 18 (*bottom*), 24 (*top*), 28 (*bottom*), 30 (*bottom*), 33, 35, 42 (*top*), 44 (*middle*), 53, 54, 56, 58 (*bottom*)

Sam Viviano   pages 4 (*top*), 5, 7, 8, 9 (*bottom*), 10, 19 (*top*), 22, 24 (*bottom*), 25, 34, 37 (*top*), 38, 42 (*bottom*), 52, 55 (*bottom*), 58 (*top*), 60

Photographic credits

Page 10: Reproduction of Edward Hopper's painting *Automat* courtesy of the Des Moines Art Center, purchased with funds from the Edmundson Art Foundation, Inc., 1958.2

Page 11: Pictorial Parade/Harold Lambert

Page 36: NASA/Science Source

Page 81: Courtesy of Pepsi-Cola Company

Page 82: Leo de Wys Inc./Nancy Kaye

Page 85: Lincoln Potter/Liaison International

Page 88: Stock Boston/Mike Mazzaschi

Page 92: Mark Antman/The Image Works

Index

The numbers in this index refer to unit numbers, not page numbers. You should also consult the relevant Grammar Summaries for each unit (on pages 66–80).